Tune into the

Magic
Within

*How to Tap in to Your Psychic Abilities and
the Art of Manifesting*

JANE VONEMAN-DUPEROW

BALBOA.
PRESS
A DIVISION OF HAY HOUSE

Balboa Press books may be ordered through booksellers or by contacting:

Balboa Press
A Division of Hay House
1663 Liberty Drive
Bloomington, IN 47403
www.balboapress.com
1 (877) 407-4847

Because of the dynamic nature of the Internet, any web addresses or
links contained in this book may have changed since publication and
may no longer be valid. The views expressed in this work are solely those
of the author and do not necessarily reflect the views of the publisher,
and the publisher hereby disclaims any responsibility for them.

The author of this book does not dispense medical advice or prescribe the use
of any technique as a form of treatment for physical, emotional, or medical
problems without the advice of a physician, either directly or indirectly. The
intent of the author is only to offer information of a general nature to help
you in your quest for emotional and spiritual well-being. In the event you use
any of the information in this book for yourself, which is your constitutional
right, the author and the publisher assume no responsibility for your actions.

Any people depicted in stock imagery provided by Getty Images are
models, and such images are being used for illustrative purposes only.
Certain stock imagery © Getty Images.

This book is a work of non-fiction. Unless otherwise noted, the author
and the publisher make no explicit guarantees as to the accuracy of
the information contained in this book and in some cases, names of
people and places have been altered to protect their privacy.

Print information available on the last page.

ISBN: 978-1-9822-0551-5 (sc)
ISBN: 978-1-9822-0550-8 (e)

Balboa Press rev. date: 05/28/2018

Tune into the
Magic
Within

Magical Experiences

We all have the ability to experience magic in our lives, paying attention to synchronicities and angelic experiences. Sometimes it is very trying to live in these times. But if you apply your inner magic to realize that by changing your thoughts and frequencies to create a vibration of joy, you can attain anything you desire, by connecting to source.

I have experienced everything from seeing blue orbs of light around me, to seeing my angel and connecting with spirit guides. I also taught myself to connect with the other side and experienced that we all have a God inside of us, capable of making anything that we desire to appear in our lives. By just asking for it, I started to notice everything I asked for was showing up in my life. We are all given this God given earthly power the day we are born.

When I started on my spiritual path after having a near-death experience and seeing an angel, I started having psychic dreams and seeing beams of light around people. I realized that there is more to life than just this earthly existence.

If you want to you can soar high with me in this book and learn how to incorporate these things into your life. Come with me on a journey to experience how you can tune into your magical frequency within, to experience anything you desire.

In today's economy find out how, with our thoughts, we can choose to either add to the struggle, or create success. I will tell you about my experience of how I tapped into my inner God and how I experienced magic beyond my wildest dreams.

A so called "weird science" and going back to my future reveals how I tapped into an inner kind of magic that created all kinds of exciting phenomena. Realizing that we are co-creators of our soul existence, follow my story, into the true life events that happened while I was least expecting. We all, as a mass of people make a joined effort with our thoughts to affect the economy and the way world events happen, even affecting the stock market and our personal abundance.

I hope you have fun with me on this journey into all the ways you can develop into a powerful spiritual being, tap into your psychic abilities and see daily signs that magic really does exist in every day life.

Chapter One

Connecting with the spirit world on the other side has been a passion of mine for a long time. The obsession began when my cousins died when I was twelve years old. They were in a fatal car accident. I was very close to them and when they died I was not allowed to attend the wake. For a long time I was in denial though I tried to go on as usual. I was a child, too, and looking back I now feel that I suppressed long term grieving and healing that needed to take place. But I did not have the tools. No one in my family knew what to do for me because they were dealing with their own pain. So I went on as if nothing happened, but I did stop flying in my dreams. I do remember that clearly.

When I turned 21, I started to feel the pain that I had pushed away resurface. Into my forties I realized that all through my life I never really faced my abandonment issues. I would prematurely abandon relationships because I was afraid they would die or leave me. I realize now that this goes back to my cousins' death.

After I realized how important it is to find closure after the loss of someone you dearly love, I made it my life's mission to help people to heal from this kind of pain. My heart drove me to make a decision to become a clairvoyant and medium. This passion was so strong that I worked night and day doing all of the things mentioned in this book's later chapters. I walked in the woods to connect with the divine source because this was always my connection with God.

Walking in the winter bundled up in the beautiful snow was a favorite of mine. I never minded being alone because this was my sacred time with just God and I, savoring every peaceful non-earthly thing I could. More or less, I wanted to bring heaven into my own existence on earth and really connect with spirit.

Immediately I set up an altar in my bedroom, by candlelight, and would turn all the lights off and just gaze at my face in the mirror in front of my sacred altar. My face would change into many facets and I started to notice that people or other entities would come over my face. Tears would roll down my eyes because I was not afraid. I knew I tapped into something.

When I would talk to people I noticed little white stars dancing around them. I know that this was probably other spirits who crossed over hanging around them. I would also see bright colors. These were colorful prisms of light that I knew were angels or auras. I continued to meditate. Living in a constant state of peace, well being and joy was the feeling that came over me out of my little altar, where I would connect with God every morning and chant powerful affirmations. I realized that heaven was starting to come to me. I was also starting to notice things about frequencies. I would be thinking something and I would get in my car to find a tune on the radio and it was exactly what I was thinking about. Or I would want something and I would think about it all week and then I noticed it would just be there.

I also noticed on the days or months when something bad happened to me and I started to get stressed, I would create fear around it and make myself physically sick. I was no longer living in the peace that I had created from my God connection. I had to work hard at getting myself back to that state of mind again. But with meditation and chanting I was be able to regain my center. By just believing and trusting that there is something greater than all of us I realized I was attaining much ancient wisdom and tapping into a higher state of being, simultaneously changing my vibration.

Angels appeared in many photos I took after I started to notice the God connection in my life. They started to appear in many places and I saw orbs appear in other photos. Angels do exist. They surround us with their holy wings of protection and protect us in many of life's situations. I started to realize that Angels were always around me, even walking earth angels who are real people with incredibly kind hearts. They help orchestrate things to happen in our lives to bring us into harmony and meet our desires. When I meditated on my angels I started to see glowing balls of light around me.

Near-Death Experience

I had a near death experience in 1991. While in the ambulance, I had an angel appear to me. She said three things to me: 1) "Patience is a Virtue," 2) "In God we Trust" and 3) "When you see a penny on the ground that is a reminder that I am with you." She also explained that some of the things the doctors were doing to me were incorrect. But she said not to worry because if you have patience you can heal yourself back to a whole perfect body. She was a black woman and had a burlap cloak. She was not what one might call a typical looking angel. But I will never forget her. This experience changed my life.

The Way We Are God

I started to notice my thought patterns. When I thought of something negative and dwelled on that thought, I seemed to attract it to me. When I focused on a positive thought, I saw that it also showed up in my life.

I realized I must keep my thoughts positive to maintain my goals of success and the things I desired in my life. Realizing that I needed to go beyond the limitations of other people's image of me, I knew that I had to get in touch with a source inside of me. That started to make things happen and turned my life around.

I was in counseling paying exorbitant amounts of money to a person that earned a degree in college and could afford to charge me $125.00 for an office visit, but was it worth me unloading all of my hurts from my past over and over again? Was I really getting anywhere?

When I decided not to go to counseling anymore and realized that my past molded me into who I am today and all the pain and drama I suffered in my life gained me more knowledge than my counselor's degree and countless years of school. I realized that the learning experience came from that lesson and that I needed to take back my life's purpose and to fulfill my dharma and soul's reason for why I was really here.

I am a psychic and I wanted to help people with my gifts. I considered helping people by listening to their problems and offering solutions while channeling a higher dimension. Trying not to judge anything or anyone anymore was helpful in the fact that I was not stuck in thinking of material things or obsessing about other people and their actions.

I just learned to move on after things happened to me and more or less turn away from it and the emotion that it caused me, so that I could attain my goal of reaching a spiritual peace or Nirvana way of thinking. I broke through the barrier of fear and dared to dream a life that I thought was never possible, realizing that it was totally possible that I created health, wealth and a multitude of abundance.

I realized that I was healing a chemical imbalance in my body due to my belief that I could heal all aspects of my body. By constantly stating every day to myself "My body is perfect," my body felt better and better.

We are getting ready to go into an era around 2012 known as the Aquarian age. The Mayan calendar ends, and my interpretation is such that the life as the Mayan people will change and the calendar of events will change around that belief. The Mayan's believe that with the Aquarian Age comes much suffering due to planetary shifts and weather changes. I pondered on the notion that the Mayans could, by the masses of Mayans, create this to happen by their thoughts...a self-fulfilling prophecy. I am convinced that a mass consciousness of thinking can actually change world events.

By my own experience with my thought process I realize that I have created everything that happens to me. I cannot control what happens to others, but I can control what happens to me and how I react to others or the way I react to myself in varied situations.

I suffered from great anxiety and fear in my life. But I realized that I was inflicting this upon myself stemming from emotional imbalance. By changing my thought processes to positive energy, I could attract positive energy and light.

Every human on earth is a divine spark of light. At the moment of conception we are pure matter and spirit. We are formed from a vibration called love which is very powerful. We continue to vibrate frequencies our whole lives. We just need to be aware of what vibration we are carrying. When we tap into a higher conscience by meditation, prayer, yoga, fasting, exercise, chanting and positive thinking we vibrate at a higher level and frequency. We can train our minds to do anything including tap into the God given gift of intuitive abilities.

Angles, spirit guides and deceased loved ones are all around us and we can feel their love, if we remain open to the signs and feelings. When I stand in my kitchen and see a beautiful rainbow that is forming like a prism of light from the sun, I stare it and appreciate the feeling of love and peace. I believe that rainbows are a sign from God. I have the mind of God inside of myself, as we all do. Heavenly dimensions are created by our powerful thoughts. We are like walking alchemists. We can even turn our thoughts into gold, literally. I will explain what I mean by this by telling you a story about while I was getting ready to go on a cruise to Mexico.

The Gold Sea Horse

I was listening to music about the sea and carrying a very happy vibration for two weeks about going to the ocean. I was singing songs about the sea and spinning around in my living room anticipating how happy I was that I was going on the cruise to Costa Maya, Mexico. I was so grateful and excited about my trip that while I was on my daily walk, I looked down and saw a pure fourteen karat gold sea horse. I was carrying such a joyful vibration all week about the sea that I created an object to appear, just by thought.

Simply by my thinking, I realized that someone had dropped the sea horse just for me to find. I began to see that we are like God ourselves. What we think, we create. I noticed that by being grateful and thanking the universe and God that I am happy with what I had, more seemed to show up in my life. Gratitude is definitely the key to increased frequency of magic's appearance.

This experience is called an a-port. By definition, an a-port is the appearance of objects in material form created by the thoughts we are thinking. An a-port can occur as well from the spirit world. Spirits can leave objects on the physical plane, when we are thinking of them.

Life is like a wishing well. Be careful what you wish for! We are all born to be happy. We are not born to be miserable. If we tell ourselves we deserve misery then that is what we create. Like a spark of electricity, we can manifest what we want by holding positive thoughts and vibrate frequencies.

I asked for release from my negative obstacles that hold back growth so I could grow. I still do this and I continue to grow.

Negative Vibrations

I went through a phase of poor health in my life. In my near-fatal car accident, I had lost my spleen. I learned that I used my accident as an excuse for weakness within myself and my life went nowhere for a while. I wasn't growing spiritually and I stayed in an illness cycle. I consulted doctor after doctor with no results and kept taking more and more antibiotics, which systematically shut down my immune system. By constantly focusing on illness as the problem and doctors as the solution I stayed stuck in fear that I had no ability to heal my own body. I carried a frequency of sickness by talking about it all the time and drawing attention to myself that way.

Never forgetting my angel, I thought constantly of her. Her skin was dark and she had messenger eyes that were trying to warn me. I felt she was warning me about going to the doctor too much and taking too many antibiotics. My angel already knew the path I had taken and that I would continue to follow it for a matter of five years. I believe that is why she told me "patience is a virtue." She knew I had to show patience and wait for the healing process to begin after I had stopped abusing my body. I started to realize that our bodies are like temples. We must take care of them. I was naïve at the time. I could have died but was given another chance to really live. This is likely another reason why I felt driven to help people and become a clairvoyant. I wanted to start tapping into my intuitive self in order to stop making deadly decisions.

Sometimes in life we don't always follow our higher self and our intuition. Nothing in life is really the wrong choice because we grow from the experience, but I want to help people to make better choices so they do not suffer. I love helping people to find solutions to their problems and providing contemporary counsel. By doing readings, I get in touch with my heart chakra.

The Radio Experience and the Clairvoyant

Soon after my near-death experience I was given a gift of tarot cards. I began reading for family and friends, always trying to keep my readings in the light and positive. I then decided I had honed my skills enough and was prepared to start working as a professional psychic and medium. When people I read for began calling me and proclaiming my accuracy and thanking me for making them feel better, I began to find validity in the notion that we all or born with a gift of intuition. I ask God and my spirit guides to work through me and help keep my reading pure from the heart and help the client to be able to identify what message spirit is giving me. My spirit guides are who initially helped me and I began building a relationship with them. A little later in this book I offer a meditation to get in touch with your spirit guides. These guides and your angels are very important.

People who need readings are usually troubled about a question about career, love life, relationships with others, financial questions and so on. When it comes to money a lot of people are worried. I always tell them that money bears the words "In God We Trust." We never really need to worry about money. The universe and God always provide it for us. We need to let go and trust.

The more meditation, chanting, praying, affirmations and believing in myself as a psychic and medium, the more my skills improved. Sometimes I fasted in the summer for a day or so and spent a lot of time outdoors. This was my connection with God. I woke every day, and still do, looking forward to life, not fearing anything that comes my way. This was and still is difficult, I admit.

One thing that helps me is realizing that life is eternal. We never really die. We just move to another dimension and our bodies become a beam of light that travels into this other dimension where there is no pain or suffering. When I was very sick this belief system helped me cope with illness and never fear it. I realized if you want to heal your body, you must love the condition and tell yourself you love yourself every day, holding on to no anger, for this is a block of healing.

Acceptance is the key to happiness in every situation. Fear holds one back from the healing process and the energy stays stuck and not able to heal. I ask my angels to help me let go of any fear or worry and negativity. This is what helped me. Later in this book I will offer a healing meditation.

Honoring My Temple

Paying attention to what I was putting into my body became an important ritual for me. I began developing food allergies as a result of all the years I took antibiotics. Essentially, I had to start over and eliminate all sugar and white flour, replacing them with lots of fruits and vegetables. I cut out caffeine and ate only white meats and eliminated red meats.

Reflecting back on my story about refining my tarot card reading skills, I approached a local book store and was hired as a reader. I was so excited about my first job as a psychic and getting paid for it. I sat many days without any customers and some people even got so mad at my readings that they raced out of the store, slamming the door behind. I started out trying to hold people's hands and putting down the cards and attempting to connect with their energies. I learned to avoid anymore of these type of angry readings because I trained myself to listen to spirit. The key ingredient during a reading is to trust that God will come through and give you the messages that the person needs to hear.

The pinnacle of my reading career's forward movement is when I started to believe that God would give me the messages. By simply stating that I was a clairvoyant and believing in myself, I acquired a successful following and clientele of repeat customers. Business improved quickly.

Another significant past memory involves visiting a doctor about a thyroid condition. The doctor told me I needed to take a radioactive pill that was filled with iodine so that it would help my thyroid stabalize. I took the pill at the hospital and left that day. On the way home I turned on the radio. I heard the song on the radio and it was playing "I'm radioactive." From that day on I paid particular attention to songs on the radio and often find that they were similar to what I was thinking. This realization dramatically improved my awareness of vibrational frequencies.

My Chanting Experience

One day while doing an old Tibetan chant, I experienced a moment of clarity and shock. This ritual was helping me to create abundance in my life. By making an Ah sound out of my third eye, and saying an affirmation "I deserve abundance and prosperity," and "I am having abundance and prosperity," I created abundance to show up. I was doing the chant about ten minutes a day for a week.

A couple of days later I had gone to a garage sale with a friend. I had decided to make some small purchases considering I did not have a lot of cash on me that day. I purchased a duffle bag for a dollar. When I got home, I opened up the bag and found $280.00 in it. I credit the affirmations for my abundance. So I started practicing this in my daily life. What we affirm, we create. I started to do things in my life to manifest abundance. I continued my affirmations ritual and found a fifty dollar bill in a shopping mall and a ten dollar bill on a trail in the woods.

I realize that I was in control of my abundance and the magic in my daily life. I realized something miraculous. I create every outcome in my life by my own thinking and by adopting a belief system that I am a powerful human being with a kind of God inside of myself. A God that helps me to be able to create the desired outcomes of my life. I started to look into other ways to magically manifest. Everything is attainable in our lives; we need to just work on ways to manifest them.

Making a treasure map was one of the things I decided to create. I hade taken a class from a local women named Evelyn. She amazed me when she said we could take poster board and put a picture of myself, in the middle. She also said all of the things that we wanted to show up in our lives, could be attained if we glued them on the treasure map. I cut out pictures from magazines, and glued them around my photo. I went back daily and looked at my image on the poster board with my cruise ship glued on; the vacation I strongly desired to have.

Around six months later my husband decided to take his income tax money and send me on a cruise with his sisters. This chic cruise was one of the most exciting events in my life. I started to appreciate the magic that my treasure map had done for me. I continue to create one for myself at least every six months.

Making a cosmic list is another method that I used. The method consists of writing my goals, hopes and dreams on a piece of blank paper and placing it under my bed. The results are the abundance that I so much desired; the manifestation of my goals, hopes and dreams. By just believing that these methods would work, they did.

Power

Starting to honor my personal power, I decided to build a power place in my home. This is called my altar. I included a variety of sacred objects on my altar such as my Grandmother's rosary and my Grandfather's special little crystal ball that he liked to look into daily when he was alive.

Sitting in front of my altar is a daily morning ritual. I feel that my altar is a great power place in my home; a place where I can get in touch with my God consciousness. This altar is my tabernacle. I commune in front of it in prayer and know that the objects I put around it or things on paper written down would definitely show up in my life.

My little altar is astounding. On one occasion when the power was out for about three days during the national black out, I grew tired of not having electricity. When I went to my altar to ask God to turn the power back on, at the exact moment that the words fell out of my mouth the lights appeared. I was a little surprised at the immediate response, but continued to roll with my magic, just laughing and telling everyone about it. I did not care if people thought I was nuts. "Yeah right, like I could make the lights go on?" That is what I am sure people thought. But I know what I experienced. Maybe it was synchronistic that I prayed at the same time they were turned back on. I don't have the answer but I respect the power of my altar.

Chapter Two

A couple of months passed. I was getting ready to take a bath one day. I had a cold that would not go away. My thoughts were becoming negative again and I was considering taking an herbal supplement. I had been on herbal supplements for many years. I now realize that I had a problem with a dependency on popping pills to feel better. At first it was the antibiotics and than the herbal supplements. The problem was the herbs started to also accumulate in my body becoming toxic and clogging my liver. I was really sick.

I made a conscious effort to get off all the herbal supplements, but then rushed right out to the doctor and had him prescribe me an anti anxiety pill. It seemed I could not escape from the belief that a pill was going to help me. I started to feel better but then became sensitive to the anti-anxiety pills. I, started to itch all over.

I remembered my angel, warning me about doctors prescribing too many things when I was in the ambulance. I was proud of myself when I got off the anti anxiety pills. This was a major hump. By eliminating all the herbal supplements my body was free of all dependency and my food allergies were miraculously clearing.

On the day that I had developed a cold and prepared to soak in the tub, I decided to ask my spirit guide for guidance. I laid out a bottle of herbal supplements on the side of the bathtub and filled my tub with the hot water. I was really struggling inside and desperate to heal my cold for it was Christmas Eve and I wanted to be well for Christmas. I looked inside of the bathtub and there was a piece of paper floating in the tub. "What is this and where did it come from"? I thought to myself. The magazine scrap had writing on it: the word "Change." I knew what my guide was trying to tell me. I did not need anything in my body to heal my cold.

This was another a-port. I started to envision my body engulfed in beautiful blue light. I remembered hearing somewhere that our bodies are eighty percent water so I focused on changing my water inside of me. Repeatedly I just decided to state over and over again, saying affirmations to myself. "I love myself." "My body is perfect." I started to cry from the magical experience with the piece of paper. I affirmed that I do have a spirit guide who was trying to help me along with my angels.

Spirits and angels always helped me in my readings with people, directing my thoughts and voices inside my head, knowing what to tell people to make them feel better.

My whole passion in life shifted to serving others; helping others with my experience was my goal.

The Lottery Ticket

Sitting in front of my power place and meditating on the word Om, was a favorite past time of mine. This word can be said seven times daily, in front of an altar. By the seventh day you will have an intuitive experience or a vision of some kind.

Another experience that I had with my spirit guide was this; when I decided to play the lottery one day. I just wanted to play the "Pick Three" and I went to the local vendor to buy the ticket. I picked the numbers 249. While I was walking out of the store I looked down on the ground and saw a piece of paper. On the paper was the number six. My mind told me I should play the number 246 instead. I did not listen to my thought and went home.

The next day I called on the phone to hear the numbers. The pick three was 246. I realized that my guides tried to help me, but I did not pay attention to my instinct.

13

The Call from My Sister

Later that month, my sister called me and said that when she left a friends house who had cancer. She was really scared that he was going to die. She got into her car and the radio was dead. She called me in a panic and said that she felt it was a bad omen and that it was a sign that he was going to die. I told her that if she was thinking about death, the radio was just a warning and that she should change her thoughts immediately and start singing and believe that the radio would go back on immediately. She hung up and called me back, within three minutes. She said she asked the radio to turn back on, and trusted that I was right. She believed wholeheartedly that the radio would go right back on. Right after that, she said the prayer and the radio turned back on. She called me so excited and told me that changing her thoughts did change her surroundings.

This was a pinnacle point in my belief of magic. I witnessed first-hand magic's effect on someone else. I was on a mission to show others that it existed. Speak and think only that which you want to appear in your life, then let go and believe in your magic. It is that simple. By speaking about what you want to create you are carrying a frequency or vibration like a radio transmitter. This works in all areas of your life including health, money, relationships, etc.

This book is intended to remind you of things that you already know inside. You can think of it as a spiritual companion. Seek you personal truth and honor your magic within to create. The state of harmony and heaven on earth is yours to attain. If you count your blessings more abundance will come. Let go of obsessing and worrying. These things are not needed in any situation. Just remember "In God We Trust." If you are grateful for the things you already have and at peace with them, more will be created.

Working with the Elements
of Earth, Air, Fire and Water

I was raking my parents leaves on a windy day. I had a blue tarp and it kept blowing closed, from the winds force. I kept trying to rake the leaves on to the tarp, but the wind kept blowing it over and it would fold so that I could not get the leaves on top of it.

I thought about talking to the wind and asking my angels to help me to make the wind stop and be still for a moment, while I raked the leaves on to the tarp. I laid the tarp flat and I spoke to the wind. To my amazement the tarp did lay flat while I raked the leaves on to it and stayed still until I was finished. I realized the power of communicating with the elements.

That day I heard my spirit guides say the words "weird science" and I laughed. I remembered an '80's classic movie where two boys made a computer generated woman into a real life person with their thoughts. They knew just what they wanted to manifest and they did it.

Life is like that for me as I continue to pay attention to all the magic that appears in my life, while focusing on it and being aware of the signs.

Back to the Future

I was walking through my house one day and my spirit guides said the name "Marty McFly." I remembered he was a character in the movie "Back To The Future,"

I quickly became busy, completely forgetting that I heard the voice from my guides until I began browsing through some old photo's of my parents.

I was gathering old photos for my parent's fiftieth wedding anniversary party. Among the photos, I came across one of my parents sitting in chairs on the beach at the ocean. We used to vacation in Myrtle Beach every year so the picture was perfect. I went up to the store to copy the photo quickly realized that I had forgotten the photo. At the store I opened the scanner. There was a photo of another couple with the exact same ocean view and the same type of chairs and beach umbrellas as in my parents' photo. I was amazed at the two photo's similarities. I removed it from the scanner and reported it to the store clerk. He thanked me and I left to get my parents' photo that I had forgotten. When I arrived home I looked again at the photo and noticed how dark my Mom and Dad were in the picture. You could hardly see their faces. I thought of the movie "Back to the Future" and how that experience was kind of similar with a different twist to it.

I believe that my guides wanted me to see the synchronicity in that event, and to have fun with it, seeing that anything is really possible. Could we change the element of time itself, to go back into our past? That is a question I asked myself.

Staying in the Power of Now

After my "Back to the Future" experience, I realized that staying in the power of now is critical. Do not dwell on your past, because we cannot change it, but we can change the way we act towards the future. I pondered this one day while looking at a beautiful sunset.

I was at a cabin for the weekend with my family at Christmas. I was memorized by the sunset's beauty. The cabin had a deck with a hot tub. Sitting on the hut tub I noticed the sunset was the color of lilac and lavender. I had never seen anything so beautiful.

I was consumed by the power of now. My mind needed only to focus on the beauty of the lavender sunset.

I firmly understood that I needed to amend my scattered thought processes and replace them with the power of now. Often I felt irritable or frustrated at life's events or at the way I felt physically. I asked the universe for help in getting to the root of the emotion that was bothering me.

The weekend at the cabin I felt out of place as far as where I fit in my family growing up. I reflected on my past and all of the mistakes I had made. I felt that my family identified me for my past mistakes and it shaped who I am today. I failed to realize that everyone in your family is exactly the personality and order system of who they are supposed to be. Similar to the alpha omega system used by wolf packs, the family hierarchy play a defining role in how we feel about ourselves as individuals. Where we fit in our family description does define who we are, but we cannot let that limit us as individuals.

In the rest of this book I am going to show you ways that you can tap into your psychic abilities by using the vibrations and frequencies that I have used. From meditation to vision questing, I will go over my experiences of tapping into my magical self and carrying a much happier vibration to achieve what I wanted in life. The reason I decided to write this was to help people who want to experience life's magical potential and how you can carry a frequency to experience it in every day life.

Meditation

When we meditate, we are seeking our contact with the creator or spirit. We can communicate with God and find the answers for ourselves and our highest good. We allow ourselves to go into the astral realms, when we meditate. By doing a guided meditation, we can become more aware of things that exist in other dimensions and use it daily to relieve stress and combat disease in the body and emotions. We tap into the subconscious mind and ease the conscious mind as well.

When gazing into an object for a long period of time, a halo forms around it. If staring into a ball of sunlight that has come through the window onto the floor, it will also become a bigger ball of light and form many colors. Mediation is simply taking a deep breath, holding for a second and than letting go. The body immediately feels much calmer.

When doing a meditation to connect with your angels or your spirit guides, you can find out who these angels and guides are that stay with you through life. I have added some meditations in this book to help you tap into this.

Our higher self always knows what to do in times of extreme unfortunate circumstances or confusion, moments when we slow down and connect to the God within. Our divine spark or light within can handle almost any experience that we may encounter. By changing our perception of how we handle tragedy, and look at it in a positive light as learning and growing experience and decipher the good in it, we can see that we do not have to fear pain or suffering.

What does not kill us makes us stronger and you can look back after the experience and be grateful for it. We all have stress factors in our life but if we learn that our minds create our existence we can recreate our lives with our thoughts to form new situations that are not so stressful.

Our perception of things is an illusion. Everything is the outcome of what we have created. By believing that the universe or world is loving and kind, we can create loving kind things to come to us.

By saying things like "Life sucks," we will create this also. Meditate in front of your power place by thinking what you want to create. Say out loud what your creation is and than chant the words "Ahhh." This works to bring things in. You will start seeing things that immediately happen in your life as a result of this manifestation meditation. It is like magic. All the Ascended Masters are around you. When you feel confused and need an answer, never worry. The answer always comes. The universe always supplies the answer to every question. It is given through other people or something you see in the news or television. Spirit always wants you to feel relaxed and sure. I say clarity three times daily if I need an answer to something. I wait, sometimes for a week, but I always hear the answer.

Free Hot Dog, One Mile

When you see a sign like this it stirs up a lot of excitement. You start to get hungry for the free hot dogs and you consider the offer. The same type of excitement and energy is how any business finds success. If you are self employed, it is the sign or advertising that creates the vibration to bring people to the free hot dogs. If we should carry this excitement in our business much success will come to us. When we are generous and help others make money, we will make money ourselves. This is called tithing. I believe tithing is very important to have more abundance. When you give to others, it comes back to you tenfold. When we are generous and help others make money, we will make money ourselves.

Surrounding ourselves also with loving positive people and not drawing our energy to the news of tragic events, sickness or suffering makes our world feel much better and we are generally happier people. I'm not advising not to love someone or care for the sick. Rather, I am saying that even in these situations blessings exist. Families grow closer or it makes them stronger.

Imagine the feeling you have on a vacation. The atmosphere is usually exciting. The blue water at the ocean glistens under the warm sun's reflections. These are energies we should hold in our daily lives in the pursuit of abundance and bliss.

In the next chapter I will explain how to tap into you intuitive abilities. There are many meditations and things that I have done to tap into my psychic abilities. This will help you on your psychic path.

Chapter Three

Angel and Spirit Guide Meditation

Now you are ready to work on the first steps in tapping into the magic within and your intuitive abilities. You are ready to meet your angels and your spirit guides.

Sit in a quiet place and imagine a beautiful light in front of you. With your eyes closed, you can pick what color you want this light to be. See this light turning into a beautiful angel that has a smile on his or her face. This angel is full of radiance and love. It is your special angel. Then imagine another being coming towards you in your mind's eye. This is your spirit guide. You spirit guide can be a male or female. It can look any way you want him to look. Imagine your guide holding outstretched arms to hold your hand and your angel is standing next to your guide. Have your spirit guide stand gently in front of you and ask your guide out loud to give you a message. Wait with your eyes still closed to hear the message. You may hear a soft voice or loud voice say something. If you don't get anything right away be patient. You will hear to voice. Keep trying until you hear a voice. This is called clairaudience or hearing from spirit. This is the first step in becoming an intuitive.

After this meditation try to develop a relationship with your guide or your angel each day. Ask your guide or your angel for signs of what their names are. One day ask your angel to speak to you and then pick another day to work with your guide. We all have angels and guides. You may receive a phone call from a stranger that meets the description of your guide in the meditation. Ask what the name is. This is sometimes the universal way of giving you your guides name. You may also pick a name that comes to you. Ask constantly for messages from your guide. Songs on the radio are ways I have connected to my guides or angels.

I was meditating a few moments before a reading. I asked for a sign from my spirit guide, if he was with me that day. I was sitting at my reading table and the phone rang. It was my Uncle Tom. He never calls me. I thought something was wrong, but then he said that he had met a Native American person and wanted to give me his phone number. My uncle knew I was interested in the Native American path so he thought I would like the number. I follow the Native American path and had, for a long time, realized my spirit guide was a Native American male named Spirit. I said thank you to my uncle and proceeded to call later that day after my reading. The woman who answered said he was asleep but he would call me back later. He never called me. I realized it was just a sign from my guide. My guide used my uncle to call me about a Native American male.

Protection

When we are in danger we may hear an overpowering voice from our guide warning us. As in the experience with my angel. Once when I was in the shower I heard a voice say "lock the door." I got out of the shower and locked the front and back door, just in case. Later that day I got a phone call from a telemarketing person that said "Are you aware that three houses get broken into in the United States, every three seconds"? I realized that this voice was probably telling me about the phone call I was going to get. I did start locking my door. I want to stress though, that we should think of the world as a loving place and disregard everything we hear on the news that makes you fear based.

I would like to site another example of messages from my guide. One day while I was going through a period of doubting myself as a reader, I got in my car and turned on the radio. The voice in the song was singing "So I guess the fortune teller's right." I just started crying because I realized that I was being comforted from my guide.

Continue to work with your guides and angels daily until you have this work perfected and you have established a close connection with them. They will be with you when you go to the other side. They will be the first ones to greet you. They will be with you for an eternity.

Now we can move on to work that I have done with ESP cards. In this next chapter I will explain what I have done with some simple cards I have made out of paper and cardboard to help me with my intuition.

ESP Cards

I want to explain how to make E.S.P. cards. These cards will help you tap into your psychic abilities. You can use a regular deck of playing cards. Lay three cards down and ask your guide to show you what card is the red card. Then pick up the card. See if you got the red card right. After you have mastered this pick up a card and hold it next to your face. Ask for a voice from your guide to tell you what the card is. Is it the two of clubs? Or is it the Knight of Hearts? Keep practicing daily. Ask your guide to show you which is the black card or which is the red card. You will improve over time and with much practice. If you do not hear an inner voice telling you what each card is, you will see a vision of some sort.

Another set of E.S.P. cards to make are moon, circle and star cards. These cards are a lot of fun! Cut cardboard into playing card size pieces. Then glue pictures or draw pictures of a moon on one, a circle on the other and a star on the last. Place these cards upside down and focus on them. Ask your guide to show you the star, then the moon and so on. Good Luck. Have Fun

Crystal Ball Gazing

A crystal ball is a psychic's tool of divination. This is a powerful tool in helping you to see visions. A crystal ball can help you develop visions and clairvoyance. Purchase a crystal of any kind. From the moment you bring the crystal home, feel unconditional love for it because it will help you in your readings. You may also leave it outside under the full moon. This will help enhance the crystal's energy. The crystal will bear its own frequency and vibration. This vibration and feeling is called psychometry. I will talk discuss this further in another chapter.

In a meditation stare at your crystal ball and then close your eyes. In your minds eye see every detail of your crystal ball while your eyes are still closed. This will help to open your third eye. Remember how the light is bouncing off the crystal like prisms of light. After a while you can do this with everything you see. When you are outside watch how the wind blows and imagine everything going in slow motion. See the beauty and magic in all things, because we are all one. When you train your minds eye to pay attention to details, you can see things on an astral plane. You can start to merge with an infinite power of clairvoyance and oneness with God. Pay attention to the world around you as if it was a slow motion movie camera. Start to describe details, speaking out loud to yourself. Be in a place of calm and peace and start to appreciate the beauty of daily living. If you realize that perception is sometimes an illusion, we can transfer our distorted negative thoughts into harmony and beauty. Observe people around you and what energies they emit, while they are walking by. Later in this book I will explain psychometry, which is picking up a vibration from a person or object. This is much needed in psychic ability. Along with something called remote viewing. The crystal ball gazing is a powerful form of divination.

Dream Journal

I would also like to discuss keeping a dream journal. This is very important when it comes to your intuitive ability. Honoring the magic in your dreams creates a whole new reality about traveling through other dimensions or astral portholes. I believe that dreams are out of body experiences. Where we go in our dreams or what we do is related to everything in your real world, but it is also a whole different existence of yourself connected to another plane. The double self or spirit self who can travel into other realms can do anything possible in dreams.

The Native Americans keep a dream catcher above their bed so that they can promote good dreams and keep the nightmares in the dream catcher. Nightmares are just healing our fears that we carry on this plane.

Dream guides are guides who help you in your dream state. Before going to bed you can ask your dream guides to give you a dream to help you understand a circumstance that is going on in your life. Also before going to sleep, keep a little crystal under the pillow that you sleep on. This represents a dream pillow. Or you can keep a little pillow made of fabric with herbs like lavender or mug wart. These are two herbs that help with divination and relaxation, and promote psychic ability.

Keep a pad or notebook by your bedside. As you sleep your third eye is going into activity. REM stage or Rapid Eye Movement starts to take place and you begin dreaming.

Psychic Dreams

I have had many powerful psychic dreams, by just keeping a dream journal and honing in on my psychic abilities. Some dreams get us ready on an emotional level to deal with things on the earth plane. These dreams prepare us for tragic events in our lives. I call these very traumatic events snakebites. The venom or medicine of these bites is so powerful and devastating that we rise up from the event and become stronger. In a shamanic belief system a snake bite is very painful sometimes deadly, but if you survive it you increase your immunity.

I had a dream once about a boyfriend breaking up with me. In the dream I was sobbing uncontrollably. When I awoke that day, he did break up with me. I felt the dream prepared me for the real thing to happen. The tears that I cried for months over Roger, my boyfriend, helped me to tap into my psychic ability so I will be forever grateful for that healing experience. I no longer fear someone leaving me or abandonment issues. Through my dreams, I had also healed that fear on a deep soul level and in other dimensions. People that come into our lives are sometimes from a past life. They can be a soul mate to help us.

I continued to have psychic dreams after this experience and kept a dream journal to honor the dream time. I kept repeatedly having dreams about celebrities. I would keep seeing things in their living room and events that would take place in their lives, before it happened. I would see what I had dreamt about the following week in the tabloids. I could not figure out why I was having psychic dreams about celebrities, but maybe it was to tell me that I was having psychic dreams. What better way to illustrate prophetic dreams than to show me people who are celebrities?

Every day record what you remember in your dreams. If you don't remember your dreams ask your dream guides to help you to remember. Light a candle the next morning and stare at the candle for a while. The dream memory may come to you. If not you can try again the next night. You will always remember the dreams you are supposed to.

The third eye or our intuitive eye is the only eye that we see through in dreamtime. Our other eyes are not used. We can see our deceased loved ones and they will come to visit us in dreams. This is a meeting with them on another dimension. If you notice how your deceased loved one looks in the dream they are usually very vibrant and happy. You are having an actual reunion with them.

I call this going to dream island. We meet our loved ones in a kind of vortex not on this plane and not on their dimension either. We meet them halfway. Start keeping your dream journal for this is very positive in honoring other dimensions and astral planes of existence from where your visionary ability stems.

Vision Quest

One of the most exciting things I did to prepare myself for more psychic visions, was a vision quest. A vision quest is a Native American custom of connecting with the creator and tapping into visionary abilities. This is regarded as sacred. It is best to be on land with trees that is far away from any roads or highways.

I was lucky to do my first quest on an acquaintance named John's property. His father was named "Two Bucks" and they were Native American. The land was Algonquin (French-Canadian) tribes burial ground. The land was first prepared by John who did a four day fast without food or water. This was in preparation for me to do my quest and to get the land ready.

When I arrived in Ashtabula, Ohio we first did a sweat lodge. The lodge is made out of branches and tarps. The four directions are honored and there is a sacred mound in the east doorway and a fire behind it. The fire has sacred rocks that heat all morning. When they are placed into a hole in the ground inside the sweat lodge, they turn a bright pink. Typically eight people sit in the lodge and pray for themselves and others. The session is made up of four different rounds. The rocks are brought in the middle by the fire keeper and the door is closed. Water is then poured on the rocks. The steam rises and the sweat begins. I'd say about five pounds of water and toxins are eliminated from the body. This is a very good cleanse and helps any kind of disease.

After the sweat, John took us down to the woods and showed me the location I would be in overnight with only an air mattress and a tarp over me to protect against rain. At first I was a little nervous because I knew I would be there all night in the dark with no tent around me for protection and the flies were really bothering me. After I blew up my air mattress and prepared myself for the long night without food or water, I put my hat and gloves on because I knew it would be cold.

This was my experience to connect with mother earth. I was alone with a beautiful river in front of me. Daylight was nice because there was sunshine so I walked around a bit. The fasting did not even bother me. This is the reason that John did his quest before me, to pray for me and to send me strength so I would not feel hungry. I had a sleeping bag and a pillow to sleep comfortably at night but John told me that I would only lightly sleep. John came down the hill once to check on me before nightfall. In daylight I looked at my reflection in the stream, I remember how full of joy and excitement I felt that I had the strength to be here in the wilderness alone.

When nightfall came, I was a little scared because there was nothing around me to protect me from animals. Dusk turned to complete darkness. I looked up above the trees and noticed beams of light flying towards me. I had no idea what they were but they stayed their distance from me and slowly flied back and forth all night over the river in front of me. When they first approached me I put my hat over my eyes so I could not see them, but then I got brave and lifted my hat a little. They were beautiful and mysterious beings or possibly orbs. I felt that they were extraterrestrial. All of a sudden I heard a noise behind me. It was a shuffle in the leaves. When you are doing a fast you will see visions. The sound was a wolf shuffling in the leaves behind me. I turned to look at it and it then changed into a tree stump.

I felt sleepy, so I pulled the covers over my head and went into a semi-twilight state. I then heard a noise like a big "woosh." I looked to see what it was but nothing was there. It seemed like a vortex of some kind of energy. It was next to my left side. I remained calm. There is something about your vibration that changes when you are fasting and you remain calm. Your connection with spirit is closer.

After a while I heard a voice out of nowhere that was deep and gruff. The voice said "what took you so long." I think it might have been my guide asking me why it took me so long to do a vision quest. My experience was powerful. The next morning I awoke from a light sleep at five a.m., and decided to make a fire. I felt proud that I survived the night of fasting.

When I returned home I had two readings scheduled at my house. They were very powerful readings because I was so connected to spirit. I will never forget my quest. I will do one again, for sure.

Letting Go of Fear and Worry

Fear and worry and lack of faith in yourself can block your intuitive abilities. Giving into fear can sometimes be a good thing. Once we walk through the fear we will remove the obstacles that block us from growth, we are elevated to a higher state of consciousness. The way to surmount fear is to honor it and be aware of its existence and then become one with it and trust that it is only an illusion. Our perception is very important. Try an exercise to help eliminate fear. Ask yourself in a situation, "What is the worst thing that can happen?" Now think of the situation and move your eyes rapidly from left to right. This is done in psychotherapy. Or I also ask my angels to help me to eliminate fear.

Connecting with Others' Energy

Before each reading I do, I hold the client's hands. This helps me to get in tune with their energy and then I will feel emotions come over me and thoughts form in my head. Sometime I will see picture in my third eye or the spirit world will form a silhouette against the wall.

A way that will help you to connect is to go to a quiet place like the library and sit and meditate on people's energy. As you see someone walk by you, try to feel any emotions that come over you; if any thoughts form in your head about the person; if you feel cold or warm. Coldness usually indicates an angry person or could be a violent or drug or alcohol addicted person. A warm feeling indicates a kind person with a good heart. This energy will feel very peaceful. Pay attention to whether they are in a hurry and what they are wearing. Let your mind start to form impressions and emotions of how the person feels. Every person carries a vibration and a frequency. While they emit this frequency, being aware and tuning into it can help you to develop the feeling called psychometry. This vibration also comes off of an object that you hold. When you get good at psychometry, you can hold an object and feel or see a vision of what emotions were stored into this object or where the object came from.

When doing psychometry in a group, people can feel objects like jewelry and get impressions in their mind. Holding an item of clothing or a ring is a great way to tune into psychometry. Hold fabric that someone is wearing and see if you can pick up where it came from. From what store did they buy it? Did they receive it as a gift? By paying attention to whatever comes into your mind will prove some level of accuracy for the first try. When you do this practice over and over, you will soon be able to pick up immediately accurate information regarding the object.

Working with Colors

Another exercise is transferring a color to someone. Have a friend sit beside you and think of a color. Have them close their eyes while thinking of that color. As your eyes are closed see if you can pick up the color in your third eye. Maybe the color will feel like something. Say the person is sending you yellow, you may pick up the sunlight or smell something citrus like a lemon. Psychometry and sending colors are two of the best ways to tune into your magical frequencies of psychic abilities.

Buying Divination Cards

Tarot cards or all forms of divination cards or essential tools in helping you to tap into your intuitive abilities. When you are reading for someone else, usually what is going on in their lives will show up in the cards. I started practicing on my own with tarot cards.

As tradition goes a person is supposed to buy them as a gift for you, so they will work better. I believe it is alright to buy them for yourself. The Rider Waite deck of cards is the most fascinating deck dating back to early times. This deck uses the Swords, Cups, Pentacles and Wands. These cards have the minor Arcana cards and the Major Arcana The Swords for instance represents strife in a person's life. Pentacles always represent money and Cups represent love. Wands have to do with change. When you start out, you can do a Russian spread. This spread is very easy and it represents past, present and future. The Celtic cross spread is a little difficult for beginners so I always used the Russian spread.

The book that comes with the deck of cards will always tell you what to do is typically easy to follow. You don't have to be college educated to understand Tarot. They refer back to Pagan symbolism. I feel that Tarot is an essential tool for a person to tapping into some form of divine energy force; To experience that magic that they really work and see that they can predict an outcome for a person or be used as a tool to help a person gain answers to a problem. To do readings for family and friends invites in the mystical side of your life and you are more aware of something greater outside of yourself. Some people feel that tarot cards are connected with evil, but this is not true. The artwork depicted is drawn from scholars many centuries old. There are stories depicted in the Old Testament having to do with Tarot and the drawings originate from the Kabala and Egypt.

The gypsies used tarot cards to see into the future and seeing into the future is why most people use tarot. The artwork on tarot is dated back to very ancient art and astrology. Angel cards are very uplifting and soothing. These are healing cards. They help the seeker to form a more positive frame of mind. Some people are scared of the pictures on tarot cards. I use both Tarot and healing cards.

After a while I put down my cards because I did not need them anymore. They were a tool and a focus. Everyone forms their own style after reading a while. New Age psychics and mediums today tend not to use cards as much. They rely more on psychometry. Mastering your skill takes years so I always tell people to start with tarot. Be patient. If you want to be a good psychic and medium you will start to realize your own style.

Before I do each reading I pray for God and my guides to send me messages that my client can identify with. I ask my ego to get out of the way. The ego is forming bias impressions or opinions about people. Once this is removed you will start to channel messages from spirit. I suggest always doing the Om sound seven times before each reading and meditation.

Sample of a Reading

Once when I was doing a reading for a young pretty female, I received a name from a spirit. The name came through very accurately. He said his name was John. I then got a feeling of violence and terrible trauma around his death. John had hung himself and his wife came to me for a reading. She was very much in pain. I got an impression in my mind of a sore thumb. I told her this and she said that John and her got into a fight the day before he killed himself and he had hurt her thumb. I realized that he was trying to say he was sorry about the sore thumb. I then got an impression of a gas station. She proceeded to say that she worked at a gas station when she got the phone call to come home.

She needed closure from John and I was the one to give it to her. Later that night I had a party where I was to read for ten people. It was in a town about thirty minutes away from where I lived. When I started reading for one woman I received a feeling that someone had crossed over. She told me her brothers name was John and that he had killed himself by hanging. I realized that this was the same John whom I had read for his wife previously that day. They had no knowledge about her coming to me. The sister of John hosted the party and the whole family was in a lot of pain over his death. I realize that spirit sent me these people to help them deal with John's death and find closure. I was amazed that is was in the same day.

The spirit world always comes through my spirit guides. I believe they give me the messages. I also think that once the guide brings them to you, the deceased person can stay in your dimension until the reading concludes. They will leave when the reading is done. How I see them is usually a silhouette against the wall or a reflection in glass. I have had spirits in full color come to me. But I have rarely seen one standing in human form. I believe that when I am ready for that they will come to me that way. I will be able to hear them speak out loud to me. The messages from them are words that I hear formed in my mind. I also get pictures from them in my third eye. Sometimes the pictures are symbols.

I was doing a reading for a young girl and I got an impression of breasts. I realized that this was symbolic and asked the girl if she was thinking of undergoing breast augmentation. She laughed and said yes.

Chapter Four

In this next chapter I will explain some stories of some readings that I have done with some of my clients.

Reading for Nancy

One of my regular clients had a father that was in spirit. The first time I read for her, I picked up an impression of a pig. I had a feeling of a Piggly Wiggly grocery store in the south, but then I got the impression of her father owning a restaurant. It turned out that her father owned a restaurant named Hoggy's. The name came through to Nancy from her father. Nancy was so grateful that her father came through and told her about the restaurant, she just about fell out of her chair. Sometimes I am as shocked as my clients when I receive such clear messages. I always thank my spirit guides. The reading for Nancy was great. It helps to have a person who is very open and not skeptical of psychics. Nancy was one of those clients. I got excited and thanked my guides for the abilities. I also had to work through the fear, though, when I realized how accurate I was. I always credit God and spirit guides for the connections to the other side and for accurate messages.

Meditation is the best way to connect with the spirit world. A large group meditation is what I highly recommend to best connect with the other side. The Om is said by everyone three times and then you wait and listen for things to come through. This works very will.

Amanda's Story

The story I am going to tell you is very important to me. One day I went to the local store to get a few things. I purchased my items and went home. On the bag was a girls face. Her name was Amanda. She had been missing for about three years and disappeared from where she was working at a local Burger King. Her face really stuck out in my mind. Out of curiosity and a passion to help I decided to go in my meditation room and meditate on this girls face. I was meditating and all the lights were off. All of a sudden a bright flash of light like a camera bulb appeared on the ceiling. I was a little spooked. All the while I was still holding the grocery bag with her face on it. I looked behind me and saw a pretty girls face appear on the wall. She had leaves around her face. I wondered if this was Amanda's spirit.

For days I could not stop meditating on Amanda. I picked up all kinds of information. I heard the word Logan County and some other information from my guides. I decided to call the police in Cleveland, Ohio where she was missing. I was very nervous. How was I going to explain that I was a psychic and medium in the Avon Lake area and that I wanted to help with the Amanda's case. I could not avoid the call, though. Something forced me to pick up the phone and dial the numbers. I started talking to the detective on the case. She was a short and to-the-point kind of woman who probably had a lot of stress in her life. I told her I was a psychic in the area and explained my experience while meditating on the shopping bag. To my surprise, she agreed to meet me at a local coffee house.

The day of the meeting with two detectives. I sat down with them and nervously drank my tea that I had ordered. I could tell at first they were suspicious of me. I showed them some credentials (an article that was featured on me as a local medium). I began by telling them some information that I received from my guides on Amanda. I felt she was upset over a break up with her boyfriend. I told them he broke up with her though. The detectives leaned forward listening to me. They knew I was correct and also knew that no knowledge was printed about that in the papers or on the news. They agreed to take me in their car to the Burger King location where she disappeared. I felt some things about her but when I felt like I told them enough, the one detective said to me jokingly "name, address and phone number would be great." He was referring to the perpetrator. I wish it worked that way but maybe it will someday. I wanted to go home and get to work on the case and meditate more.

As time went by I went out for coffee with some ladies from my church and told them about my experience. This is where the synchronicity comes in. The one woman whom I'd met that evening just happened to be one of Amanda's high school teachers. Amanda also had the last name of my cousins who died in a car accident (Marcia and Mary Kay). There were some synchronicities for sure on this case and myself. It seemed like God or Amanda's spirit or my guides would not let me forget about Amanda.

Time went on until the very same day that I wrote this paragraph. I woke up in the morning and started thinking about Amanda. It was February 12th, Lincoln's Birthday. Lincolns birthday always meant penny day to me, since Lincoln was on the penny. The connection with my Angel was about pennies when I had my near death experience, as I explained in the previous chapters. On Lincoln's Day I decided to look on the Internet for Amanda. I Googled her and I could not believe what the next day was. A song came on the website "Happy Birthday to You." The next day was Gina's birthday (February 13th). She was another girl that went missing within three weeks of Amanda's disappearance. She was last spotted on a pay phone only about a block away from the Burger King location. It was Gina's Birthday. When I started meditating on Amanda I revealed information about Gina that was very synchronistic.

When I was meditating in the morning I received a big movie screen picture of a car. The car was old and looked like a Ford Thuderbird. The paint by the driver side was dark and the rest of the car was white. Was this accurate information from my guides? Is this what the car looked like that the perpetrator was driving?

I decided to keep meditating and not do anything about it yet. I chose to pay attention to the signs. I wanted to help with her case. To sum up the story, I really wanted to help with the case and the universe made it possible that I could do just that. After a while I stopped getting any response from the detective about the case. I had the vision of the car and actually felt I had picked up some license plate numbers. I kept calling the detective but she never answered the phone. One day I had got out my spirit dice. These dice were something I invented myself from words on dice that are letters of the alphabet. I rolled the dice one day and it spelled out perfectly the name Amanda. I asked Amanda's spirit to help so that the detective would answer her telephone. I told Amanda that her spirit needed to make it possible so that I would be able to give the detective the car description and the plate numbers. After I said that little prayer, the detective answered the phone immediately. I told her the information, with tears in my eyes.

Meditation Circles

The best way for me to connect with the other side is through meditation in a circle. There is something about a guided meditation with an experienced medium or teacher that really helps you to grow as a medium. Ideally, find an experienced medium that holds classes in your area. But if you cannot find a medium then here is a sample of a group meditation that you can try in your home.

Start by turning off the lights. It helps to hold the meditation at night. Burn a candle in the middle of the room and have everyone sit comfortably. Tell everyone to breathe deeply and relax. Once relaxed everyone should chant the Om sound three times. Chant this together in harmony with one another. Then have everyone visualize a beautiful color. Imagine this color is coming around everyone and forming a beautiful protective bubble. After everyone visions themselves in this bubble they can imagine all of their deceased loved ones standing in the middle of the room. Then sit silently and listen for a word or message from loved ones. You may hear a message that does not make any sense. Sit and meditate for a while and then have a group discussion about the meditation afterward. Let each person speak about what he or she received in their meditation, and if they heard any messages. They can describe what color their bubble was and how they felt. Each person should really listen while the other is explaining anything about their meditation. See if anyone received a message for someone in the circle afterwards, by going around the room explaining each individual's meditation and perhaps someone picked up a message for someone else.

Keep repeating this group meditation at least once a month. You will improve your ability as a medium. After a while your universal mind will realize other ways of bringing in your psychic gifts. The more you practice on other people and feeling their energy the better psychic and medium you can be.

Elevating to Your Higher Conscience

To get to a level of being a spiritual master you have to come from a higher chakra at all times. Sometimes this is hard because of things that happen in life to upset us. These vibrations are like shock waves that throw us off kilter. But to come from a place of non-emotional attachment is called a state of nirvana or peace. The Egyptians call it Ma-aht; To live in harmony and hurt no one. Judging others or lack of it is a difficult way to live but to get to a cosmic level of true happiness is important. Native American's say to speak truth about people but only the good. This has been very difficult for me but I am mastering it.

When a person is judged he or she usually reacts by feeling vulnerable or snapping back at the offender in defense. To master a constant state of peace so that you will not be prone to depression, try this experiment. When someone states something to you or about you that you do not like, just look at him or her calmly and say "I'm sorry you feel that way." If he or she is judging you or trying to tell you how to live your life, that is their opinion and the way they feel. For you to not vibrate that feeling onto you so that they cannot affect you, you need to know that what they think about you does not matter. Worrying about what others think of you can destroy your happiness. By staying calm when someone is judging you, you then remain in control and have a higher frequency and vibration, so the words they state can be dismissed. You will be respected more. Another way to do this is by just stating your opinion, but showing no emotion. The emotions you may feel may be awful but eventually you will reap the benefits and get much respect as a human by remaining emotionally detached from other people's comments or remarks about you.

By doing this your ego is not getting involved, because the ego is coming from fear and a lower vibration. EGO stands for easing God out. If you drop something right away that upsets you and let God take care of it you will continue to come from a higher vibration. A person then has no power over you. This is a good way to start to elevate yourself to a level of an ascended master. You will remain at a higher energy level and will be good for your clients in readings and in helping people, instead of letting all the little petty things in life and quarrels with others drain you and cause you to be depressed and low energy.

Ask your guides and angels to help you to be emotionally detached so little things do not upset you. It is alright to grieve over a loss or death of someone. Grief is totally different.

Chapter Five

In this next chapter I want to explain a chakra meditation. The chakra system was developed in the Kabala. The Jewish mystic religion designated it, by seeing that every portion of our body has energy. If any of these energies are out of balance illness and disease will manifest. By doing a chakra healing meditation we can bring mind, body and spirit in harmony with each other.

Red

Sit comfortable in a chair or lay down for this meditation. Relax and take a deep breath. Imagine a red light coming into your sexual area and lower intestinal area. This is your Root Chakra. It controls weight issues and feeling fearful or anxious when out of balance. This area is located at the base of the spine. Imagine this red light going into your sexual organs. This is your life force and when in balance it is called the Kundalini or life force area.

Orange

Next send an orange light down through your intestinal area. This chakra controls our emotions lower digestion. When out of balance we will have feelings of being over attached to someone or something. Meditate on this orange light all through your lower stomach area and your naval area, filling all of the organs around that area. This can be a burnt orange color filling that section.

Yellow

The solar plexus chakra is the yellow chakra. When this is out of balance digestion will be affected and controls diabetes, chronic fatigue, digestion disorders and the emotions are anger, domination and aggression. When in harmony and balance there is a feeling of good heath and inner peace.

Send a glowing and soothing yellow light to this area and feel it filling all of your intestines in and around your digestion and your feeling around food and elimination. Let this feeling warm your stomach area and be at peace with life.

Green

The Heart chakra is the green light that you can visualize penetrating deeply into your heart. By absorbing this green healing light you will help your heart to be at peace and not feel inner turmoil or pain. Feeling of loss or grief will make your heart chakra out of balance. To help it heal and get back in balance you will feel confidence and compassion, send this green healing light to work on your heart chakra.

Blue

Next imagine a blue light going into your throat area. Absorb this glowing light into your throat area. This is called the Throat Chakra. When in balance, this heals areas of communication and expressing yourself confidently. When out of balance this affects the thyroid and you will have fear of expressing yourself. This also affects that area around the neck and jaw. Send this radiant blue light into this area and relax.

Indigo

The third eye chakra is the color indigo; A bright turquoise blue. This area controls your third eye. When in balance you are intuitive and clairvoyant. When out of balance you are not listening to your gut and what it may be telling you. Headaches are common with an out of balance third eye chakra. It affects vision and eyesight. It also affects the memory and sinus area. When healthy we should have clear sinus and breathing.

Imagine an indigo colored light piercing through your third eye. This is the chakra for psychic abilities and dreams. When out of balance we will have nightmares.

Violet

The final chakra is the violet Crown chakra. This is the chakra for your intuitive abilities also. Imagine a violet light going through your crown area. When out of balance you will feel confused. When in balance you will have clear intelligent thinking.

Send a violet light through your crown area. Imagine what violet might smell like. Think of it swirling all around your head. Have fun with it.

Now that you have done this chakra meditation you will feel cleansed and ready for more growth spiritually. Pay attention to your dreams after this meditation. Sometimes you will notice colors in the dream. These will be colors of the chakra system.

Wearing Power Colors for Success

Even if a person is nervous about going on a job interview, but wants to make a good impression, there are some things you can do to strengthen your aura by wearing power colors. The aura is a shield of light around us that is usually seen by a psychic or medium. We all have one and if our aura is weak it can be strengthened. By soaking in a hut tub of epsom salts or sea salt and lavender and putting a rose quartz crystal in the bath tub, helps decrease stress and empowers the aura.

Each color has an element of earth, air, fire or water, so I suggest wearing colors having to do with the elements. Yellow is bright and sunny. This color is highly active to get other people in a good mood and also the person who is wearing it. It brings a ray of sunshine with it.

Green is an earthy tone especially bright pea green or mint green and is very soothing. Men can wear this color in their ties or shirts. It helps with abundance because it is the color of money.

Red is very striking and is related to the element of fire depending on the day of the week that it is worn. This color is best worn on Tuesday as a power color. It is connection is to the astrological sign Scorpio and the planet Mars.

Black is always to be worn on Saturdays. It is a classic look and the power color for Saturdays. You will create more power around you when wearing this.

Silver or white can be worn on Mondays. This has an angelic appearance and can represent the start of a new fresh beginning to the week.

Purple and royal blue are the power colors for Thursday and are connected to the planet Jupiter and for knowledge. Purple and royal blue bring out a person's passionate side.

Orange and grey are power colors for Wednesday. They link to the angel Raphael and the planet Mercury and the sign of Virgo.

Light Blue is very healing and calming. It can be worn on Wednesday as a power color. It associates with the male energy and new birth.

Carrying Tokens for Success

Putting some sort of token in your wallet that represents drawing in money or abundance is a good idea that has always worked for me.

Carrying around a coin or something that symbolizes making more money affects the way that money comes to you. If you carry a blank check that is written out to yourself stating how much you would like to make the following year or put the deposit in your check book of how much you envision being in your account, you will see that money arrive. Carrying a gold token or a piece of laminated paper with symbols related to money in your wallet is a reminder for you that abundance is coming. Remember to never worry about lack because this will close off your abundance. Always affirm "I am having abundance and prosperity," or "I deserve abundance and prosperity."

Time and Space

Time and space are important factors when practicing divination. If you look out the window when you wake up in the morning, the sun may be reflecting beautifully on the snow or in the spring you can hear the birds chirp. Try to be aware of things slowing down and look at them in slow motion. See every detail of things that are happening around you. See the beauty of the sky and notice its color.

In this next section I will discuss Nature and the Cosmos and honoring the moon and stars; the great outdoors that Creator has given us and its vast beauty; the magic and power of the sun and solar system and of course the moon.

Next I will discuss how to do a full moon meditation. By honoring the magic of the moon, you will begin to realize that there is power around the moon. Police forces really do mark this on their calendars, because they know that there will be more crime and violence. Pay attention to the way you feel during a full moon. Do you feel agitated? Do you notice the power around the day that you are having? Are people around you upset or nervous?

The pagan religion is always known to practice ceremony around a full moon. This helps the spells and things they pray for to increase. They believe it is a time or power that is greater than other times.

During a waning or waxing moon the power of the moon is also important. If you want to manifest something, this is the time to do so. When you say affirmations, watch the power of these around a full moon or waning or waxing moon. Be careful of your words for they create your actions and your actions create your character. Your character creates your existence.

Full Moon Meditation

Now I will explain a full moon mediation. We can actually draw down the power of the moon, by staring at it. Moon gazing is an ancient art that pagans believe that they can draw down the power of the moon into their bodies and divination tools. This has been used for many centuries, to help people with their intuitive abilities.

As you begin, go out on a night that you can see the moon very clearly. A full moon is good but you don't need a full moon. If you are under a full moon, first pay attention to the face on it. Stare at the face and make contact with it as a being, as if human. Start to notice prisms of light bouncing off of it. If you are sitting in a comfortable chair in your back yard or wherever you have chosen, relax and draw the moons energy into your third eye by closing your eyes after you stare at it and feel it absorbing into your third eye. If you want you can bring out your crystal ball and lay it on the ground to absorb the energy also. See the moon energizing the crystal and charging it with energy.

If you stare at the moon long enough there will be a circle of light that forms around it. Imagine in your minds eye, your body flying up and sitting on the moon. This is a form of astral travel and some people have been known to leave their bodies and travel to the moon. They experience standing on the moon. The lucid energy of the light that the moon and other planets emits can reveal a lot about our Creator. This light is different than the solar light because it does not effect your eyesight. You can stare at it for as long as you want.

The planet Jupiter is the planet of knowledge and the planetary alignment affects our economy and the masses of people.

By our thoughts we can draw in the power of the moon's energy to help us manifest in our life. By paying attention to the moon's waxing or waning periods, you can start to align yourself to the moon's energy when you notice it's affect or vibration on your body and how you feel.

I heard a story of someone who stared at the moon all night. By morning they were seeing the dead. This may be possible. The person was already open to this and the moon brought out his or her gifts.

If you are ready to see the spirit world, they will let you see them. I do believe small children and young teens see this often. If they have had a grandparent die, they will often see them sitting in a chair or at the end of their bed at night. The deceased will appear in full color as if trying to connect with them. This is an actual visit of your loved ones. There is nothing to fear because they cannot hurt you.

When I was about fifteen, I saw my deceased grandfather. He was sitting in a chair in the living room of my house. I only saw him for a split second, but it was enough to make an impact on me. I always remember that experience. I was afraid so I blocked my ability to see anyone in the spirit world for a while after that experience. They will not come to you again if you are afraid of them, but when you meditate and open your third eye again through the exercises in this book, you may find the ability to see them.

Beings or orbs of light and colored balls floating in the room are daily experiences for me. I personally had to give up drinking a lot of caffeine. I think this can block your gifts but everyone is different. Some people can drink coffee all day long and still tap into their intuitive abilities. But I am very sensitive to it. A friend of mine named Tim, who works as a medium and psychic drinks coffee all day long. I can only imagine the visions he may have if he gave up caffeine. He has been working as a psychic and medium for thirty years. Some people need the caffeine to keep their gifts at bay. In this next chapter I will speak about chanting. Chanting is another way you can help to increase your third eye and more or less wake it up.

Chanting

Chanting is another way to help you to draw a vibration around you and make things happen. We can manifest our personal connection with our higher self. The sound Om is very powerful. When you do the Om sound each day for seven days you will start to see things change around you. You will hear and become clairaudient and be connected to messages from your guides. Just walking around your home you may hear a quiet voice repeat a message to you. The voice will keep repeating the message until you pay attention to it. This is what the Om sound can do. It also opens up your third eye and you may start to have visions. You are vibrating at a higher level of conscience and are able to connect with the Ascended Masters. In Yoga there is a chant Ong Namu Guru Dev Namo. This is a Yogi term for "I am the personal truth." Yoga is very beneficial in cleansing toxins from your body and relieving stress. When I started to do yoga I noticed a big change in myself and I felt more grounded but more aware and open. It put me in a peaceful meditative state and made me feel that I could handle anything that comes my way.

Another chant that works very well is to sit in front of your altar and say the affirmation "I am having abundance and prosperity" and then make an Ahh sound out loud. Repeat this affirmation several times daily. This will help draw in abundance in all ways; not only with money but with happiness and attracting lots of positive people in your life. You will draw in lots of fun situations also. Someone may call you and say they have free tickets to a play or the theater. This chant has worked very well for me in my psychic abilities also. I will sit in front of my power place and chant "I am psychic" and than follow with the Ahh sound. I will than say I am clairvoyant, clairaudient, clairsentient. These terms are widely used in determining what type of psychic you are. Clairvoyant means sight and visions or an inner knowing. Clairaudient means you work with sound and hearing. You will hear messages from spirit. Clairsentient means feeling. You are an intuitive that more goes by your feelings or empathic, meaning you pick up on others emotions around you.

I also use the affirmation "I am healthy and strong, I am beautiful and loved." This one helps me to feel really good about myself everyday. Try this affirmation and watch it to help your whole immune system.

Chants and affirmations are very beneficial. I once heard of a women who had cancer and wanted to heal her body, so she went around every day saying out loud to God, "Thank you for my healing." She just let go of fear and trusted that the healing would take place, and it did. She was healed from her cancer in full.

Magical Ways to Heal

Reiki is one of the most powerful ways to tap into a healing force that will raise your body's vibration to its full healing potential. It allows you to heal yourself and others by the laying of hands on the body. It was developed in Japan in the early 1900's.

Reiki is very easy to learn and use. There is an attunement that a person receives to be able to practice Reiki and once the person is attuned to it, they are able to heal. This universal life force energy is something we all have. We just need to be reminded so it is helpful to find a Reiki course in your area.

Some churches have Reiki practioners and all Unity Spiritual centers are aware of practitioners. There are Unity Spiritual Centers usually in every state and in various cities. By sending golden rays of light through your body every day and by taking about twenty minutes a day to an hour each day to do this can also heal the body. By getting some meditation CD's and listening to them while sending colors through the body and by imagining a humming vibration, you can heal anxiety and stress, and many emotional and physical disorders of the body.

There are stuffed emotions that go along with every illness that has manifested in the body weather it is cancer or arthritis. Usually the emotions are buried so deeply that they start to destroy the cells in the body that can cause disease to manifest. By getting in touch with these emotions and releasing them, we can stop holding the sick energy in our body. It is really the power of the mind that takes us out of illness. Also by cooperation on our part to change the diet and eliminate things in our life that cause stress and suffering. It is important that we treat every living soul as equal and to not hold resentment towards others, especially judgment towards others. If we respect our path and the path of others, we can get rid of judgment and realize that God works in all of us.

Manifesting

In this paragraph I would like to speak again about manifesting what you want in your life by telling you a story about a friend of mine who I will call Susan. Susan always believed that God was a punishing God and would seek his revenge on everyone that hurt her. She would always talk about God getting even with everyone that hurt her. She would focus on this constantly. She was clearly in a lot of pain.

I do realize that if someone hurts you, the best thing to do is to forgive. Holding onto the anger is like swallowing poison and waiting for the other person to die. It only hurts you. There is a thing called Karma though and what other people put out there to others does come back to them. For instance if you hurt someone it comes back to you depending on an apology. If you apologize then you are allowing the vibration to change. It is different if someone kills someone else, but usually that person pays for it, too. Internally it could eat away at them for years if they did not confess.

Going back to Susan, she was always thinking negatively and would talk about being tested and always spoke of the devil. I started to notice that she was drawing a lot of negative situations in her life, but all the while saying that God was testing her. She went through so many tests it seemed to drive her to the brink of insanity. What you focus on magnifies, these are very important words to tell you.

Susan continued to judge people and tell them that they were living their life in the wrong way and that God was going to punish them. I noticed people in her life who were supposed to be close to her, family, her parents and her own children all alienate from her. It seemed like she was trying to live a life of prayer and Christianity but all in the name of God. Susan continued to stay a victim. I continued to pray for her, but realized that I needed to let go of trying to help her realize what she was doing.

This story can make you aware of the power that we have over our lives and our happiness. We create our existence by our thinking. Think positive and trust in God. Susan was always trusting in God but she needed to align herself with the thinking of the Holy Spirit. God does not go around judging people and if we want to live like that and become a victim that we will surely create our own inner suffering until we hit the bottom.

We are truly here to enjoy life. Life can be disappointing at times and especially when people die. If a loved one dies, we have no control of the pain that we feel. But what always helped me is knowing that we really have never lost that person. There spirit always remains with us.

When we think of dying ourselves, it can seem pretty scary. First of all we do not want to leave the ones we love and secondly we don't want to suffer. If you let go of fear and realize that we are a being of light that will just travel to another dimension and that we will see our loved ones from the earth plane very soon, the fear subsides. We actually just cross over to another dimension and the transition is done in a way that we do not feel grief when we are preparing our light bodies to return home. Angels will come to assist us immediately and we will be so happy to see our other loved ones who have already passed that we forget our pain. Once we are on the other side we have no attachments to the emotions and people that we have here on this plane of existence. Our emotions of earthly attachments are healed and we come from a place of total love and happiness.

We actually change our vibration yet again, to match the vibration of the heavenly realms of existence. Every second we are here, we should only stay in the power of now and not focus on the fear of loss and death. All we have is the power of now. In the back of our minds, though, we really can know that we will just go from one plane of existence to another so rapidly that we will not feel loss or grief. What I feel people fear the most about death, is suffering. They do not want to suffer and be ill with cancer or some other malady. If we focus on this suffering we can create our own suffering in the moment we are focusing on it. The feeling is only a distorted illusion and fear of what is to come in the future.

Orb in my medicine wheel

Angels that appeared under the water falls.

Cloud formation

Chapter Six

The reason why psychics can predict the future is because, past, present and future all co-exist on one plane of reality. The ability to predict something before it happens or to predict something that has not happened yet but will happen in the future is basically the same thing that happens with a basic deck of tarot cards. Psychics live in a world where the mundane matches the mystical and they work together through time and space. The material world is not relevant to the world that a psychic inhabits. The conscious mind is related to the past and future. A reader is gathering a vibration off of someone especially when holding there hand or a picture. But a trained psychic does not need to get information off of anything. If you want to gather information about a coat that someone is wearing try holding the coat and meditate on the messages that come through on the coat. For instance if Aunt Sally bought the coat, a name may come through.

When I have practiced for years with a regular deck of tarot and doing readings for people, I started to see that the cards were showing me information about the client regarding past, present and future. I would get calls saying I was accurate on predictions. I would then put down my cards and start to meditate on things for which I needed information.

Four levels of the human psyche exist:

1. The Spirit
2. The Mental level

3. The Astral being
4. The physical body

We all have a spirit within us that is part of the divine, part of the higher realm of existence. We cannot totally understand our divine nature, but we know that all of us have a higher conscious. This is our source of inspiration that connects us to all other human beings. We are all connected by what created us. We are all one, just as past, present and future. To be a good psychic and medium you must trust this part of yourself and know that you are divine. You must trust that the information is coming through accurately. Trust in The Great Spirit giving you the information correctly. And lastly trust in your spirit guides and angels. Without them and the Creator I could not be a good psychic. But you need to trust.

The astral part of our being is an outer shell that protects us. It is an auric field that cannot be seen. It is the part of our body that has spirit and matter around it. This is our connection to the higher realms and helps us to make it to the other side when we pass.

The mental level is our creative side and left brain, right brain thinking. Our right brain is the side that is connected to the paranormal and spirit world. It is our spiritual side that connects with all human beings and is aware that we are all one. The left brain is our analytical side that knows how to learn in school. It is probably the side we use more often.

Our physical body is where we feel pain and emotions. We have these until we cross to the other side. We can use our physical senses to be in tune with smell and taste and all of the other senses. This helps with our extra sensory perception.

With the combination of all these levels of the human psyche, we are able to feel things and see things that don't appear to the naked eye, unless tapped into.

I will give you an example of what happened to me when I was in a meditation and I heard a name of a man. I happened to be working on solving a case of a missing girl who I have talked about in previous chapters. I knew that someone had probably murdered her. I heard a name and told the police the name of the man that my guides had given. Six months later I went to the drug store and was given a free newspaper. I usually don't get the news but happened by synchronicity to get one that day.

I got home and read an article in the paper about a guy that killed someone and was going around bragging that he robbed a store and shot an elderly man that was the owner. The name of the man came up in a meditation. It was the same name my guides had given me, the same name that I had received six months prior to the date in a meditation. My guides were trying to give me information about a murder in advance before it happened. I just needed to ask my guides to give me the rest of the information correctly I realized later that they were giving it to me if I had just paid attention to more details and signs around me. The universe always gives you what you desire and need.

Developing Your Intuition

After I had developed myself for a while I began seeing people's Aura's. An aura is a person's astral light that shows outside of their body. It is an energy that you can see in visible form. There are five levels of our Auric Senses or intuitive senses:

Seeing—Clairvoyance
Hearing—Clairaudience
Feeling—Clairsentience
Smelling—Clairolorance
Knowing—Claircognoscente

After you develop your abilities to see and hear by working on your psychic abilities, you will be able to see people's auras. This is one of the first things I started to see around people after I started tapping in and meditating.

Pam's Reading

While I was reading for an older woman named Pam, her husband came through very powerfully. We were sitting at my table and I was trying to channel her deceased husband. Her husband was a fire fighter and he first showed me an American flag to get my attention. I see symbols or pictures in my third eye. I gained this ability after two years of meditation. All of a sudden during Pam's reading my doorbell rang and it would not stop. It continued to ring for about three minutes when I had to stop my reading and walk out of the reading room into the kitchen and look at the doorbell box on the kitchen wall. I asked my son to take it down, so I could go back to my reading. I decided to look outside first to be sure there was no one at the front door. The doorbell button was pushed in and when I looked at it, the doorbell stopped ringing. I returned to the reading and I told her that I believed her husband had just let me know he was here and wanted to enter the house. Her husband always lived by the bell being a firefighter. This was definitely a sign for me that spirits do try to manipulate electricity so that you can see they are trying to deliver a message. This was a wonderful and quite intriguing experience.

Any time I have a reading like this I journal my experience so that I can reflect on it at a later date.

This picture reminds me of a past life. I had an experience in my life in a place like this one and it was a very good memory. We all have past lives and I would like to talk a little in this book about the feelings you may have in your life that trigger past life memories or fears.

In the next chapter I will go over past lives and how when you are giving a reading for someone, a past life memory or name may come up in the reading. If you are doing a reading for someone as I have and things are coming through that the client cannot relate to, this could be a past life connection.

Chapter Seven

Past Lives

I started to pay attention to readings where nothing came through accurately. My spirit guides sometimes give me accurate names of people in the reading. Especially people who the seeker is close to. When a name comes through that is not accurate or a name that the person does not recognize this could be a person connected to a past life. It could also be someone the person is going to meet in the future.

We all have past lives. I struggled to believe in that for a while but reconsidered after reflecting on my fear of bridges. When someone who's opinion I respect told me it might be connected to a past life memory of falling over a bridge, I had to take a look at myself and change my beliefs in past lives.

When you meet someone and you feel an instant connection with them, immediately, I feel that this is from a past life connection. If you feel that they are a relationship that you really want to be in but it just does not seem right or feel right, this is probably a person from your past life. Or if the person brings up great fear and issues for which you need healing, this could also indicate a past life relationship. When you are reading for a person, you don't need to really focus on past lives too much. That is best left to the past life regression hypnotherapy specialists. But if a name or a feeling of a place presents itself that the person cannot relate to, this is possibly from a past life.

There are a lot of experts in past life information. I do not dwell on this theory because I feel that people want to connect with this life that they are in. This life is hard enough at times. The point I want to make clear is that if you have a definite fear of something know that it probably is due to something happening to you in your past life. Why else would you fear it? We fear the unknown but we also fear traumatic events in our lives or past lives.

Fear stands for "False evidence appearing real." Fear is not to be trusted, it is only an illusion. Know that you can let go of any fear and just relate it to your past. The reality is that it will not happen to you in your future unless you think of it daily and try to create it with your thought. Thoughts are things. They create your reality. Your words create your life. Your actions create your character. Your character, thoughts and words create your future. This is very powerful.

Chapter Eight

I was doing a reading for a woman and I heard the name Angus. She started to cry and say it was her pet's name. I felt the energy of a dog in the room and actually saw something dark appear around the floor by her feet. I knew that this dog, Angus, really wanted to come through for his master. Animals are always very happy spirits. They don't care what you do to their fur once they have crossed. But any trappers know that animals should not suffer. Anyone who harms animals experiences karma or is a really sick person. I support the PITA organization, but I also think that it is OK to have animal furs. If you already own the fur you do not need to get rid of it.

We need to take care of everything around us. We are all one. The plants are nature spirits and the rock people are stone spirits. I realize that they are all spirit. I needed to be one with all of life. We must honor and protect Mother Earth for she needs us to treat her better. The environment is showing signs that we have abused her. The pollution is hurting the ozone. I don't like to focus on negative so I am saying that we should hold the energy and envision a cleaner earth. We could also hold the energy for the earth of peace and non-violence.

Cosmic Relationships

Many of us feel that other life exists in the universe. There are other planets and dimensions just like the other side. The Native

Americans believe that we originate from the stars, or star people. Yoga has a hand position that helps you to connect with knowledge from the planet Jupiter. I believe in mediation holding your thumb and forefinger together so that you can create this knowledge. Chanting may strengthen the experience. There are other planets and other dimensions. Our inter-galactic relationships do exist and they will have their moment to speak to us. The government is aware of these beings and the Pope has spoken about this also.

I once read for a man that said he believed he was abducted by an alien. He said something pulled him out of his bed when he was a child. Many people who have been interviewed about abductions state that they remember a surgery and some implant in their bodies. I keep an open mind to all possibilities. As a reader you must stay open to everyone's belief system including cosmic relationships.

The Universe is sacred, infinitely large and vast. Some of the sacred mountains in Tibet have been destroyed much like the rainforests. We see changes as a result of this in the earth's atmosphere. This is an important time right now for light workers or psychics. The veil is thinning between this earth plane and the other side. So it is thinning too between other life forces. Your focus is the bottom line. We can prepare for the changes in 2012. We can literally create a heaven here on the planet eventually if you hold this energy for the earth's environment. You must honor that magic too within yourself. Trust in the creator or the Great Spirit.

Seances and Table Tipping

Personally I don't see anything wrong with having a séance to help improve your medium skills and your psychic connection to the spirit world. You have to prepare yourself mentally to see a spirit in full color and maybe even get a vocal message from someone from the other side, when you are trying to hone in on your medium and psychic abilities. I have had spirit come to me in full color. One small toddler boy came to me and tried to get my attention by pulling my leg. He was in full color and was very happy and laughing. I was a little caught off guard by him and did not expect a visit from the other side. They usually come when you are least expecting it. If you try to push it or are afraid they will not come to you. When you are in a really lucid and relaxed state is when they will come, or also if you are happy in your life. Spirits come to happy people. If you are depressed or very sick and exerting a lot of negative energy they will not show themselves to you. But on the other hand some may come no matter what frame of mind you are in.

When I do a lot of my reading especially in someone else's home I see what I call wispy people against the wall. It is like a shadow of a person but I see if their hair is long or short, light or dark, male or female. After you do readings for a while and you start to pay attention to what is around you, you may notice some of these things coming to you. You may start to see silhouettes of people against a glass window or a reflection or spark of light. You may see full color balls floating in the air. These are angels.

Once while going to sleep I saw the portrait of the Mona Lisa floating above my bed. I still to this day do not know why I saw her. The only connection at the time was the movie the "DaVinci Code," which left a big impact on me.

Séances

A séance is usually performed with a group of people that hold hands around a round table. I am going to list the materials needed for a good séance:

Materials needed:

Round table or very comfortable sofa.
Darkened room
Tape recorder
Three White Candles

Incense : mainly cinnamon, sandlewood and frankincense.

At least three people; one medium

The prayer of protection needed before a séance is to be said before the séance starts. Everyone should sit and meditate first and say the Om seven times. The prayer of protection could go like this:

Oh Heavenly mother father God we ask that you grant us protection. Please put a protective circle of the white light of the holy spirit around us during this séance. Help us to connect with beings of light and love and keep any negative energies away from us. Grant us peace Oh heavenly mother father God. Amen.

After the prayer you want to say the chant over and over again in a group.

Beloved (state name of person that you are trying to contact), we ask that you commune with us and move among us.

You want to recite this with the whole group over and over again until you feel you have said it enough. You can ask the named person who you are trying to connect with us to rap once or send a signal that the named person is trying to connect. Ensure that the tape recorder is on or turn on a radio and switch the radio to pure static. You may hear an energy in the static change. Afterwards you can play your tape recorder. Having a séance is supposed to be fun. Do it with fun intentions.

After having a séance I started to notice different things happening in my house. The lights would just turn off by themselves. It is alright to ask the spirits to leave if you are too afraid. They will respect and honor what you want.

Table Tipping

Table tipping is just another word for a séance. An example of this is a story about a male friend that I used to date before I was married. His name was Scott. Scott would come over just to have mini séances. I really looked forward to his visits and we would get a small round table big enough to fit one candle and some incense. We would hold hands and say the chanting and prayers needed. We started to notice the table shaking and vibrating. I have heard of people who experienced the whole table rising in the air. I believe this is the energy that the participants are putting into the séance. The power of the spirit world is amazing. Spirits help coupled with earthbound help can cause things to move. This is why you hear stories of things flying in the air. The spirit world is gentle. They will not harm you. There is no such thing as the devil or evil spirits. In this next chapter I will talk about my experiences with nature spirits and the power of a group of woman with these elements: the elements of earth, air, fire and water.

Chapter Nine

There is nothing more powerful than a group of women getting together for the highest good. The mother goddess is the earth mother and our bodies bleed to give of ourselves back to the earth. We cleanse and we can birth babies. So of course the women would have much power. The old ancestors who were midwives and healers were pagan women and man came from across the waters and said that they were witches. This connection was wrong because they were not evil with their powers and spells. They just wanted to help people.

The Salem witchcraft trials had to pay back the victims' families thirty years later. The assailants assumed the female victims were practicing magic and holding the power of their cauldron. There is nothing wrong with what these women were doing. They were innocent. We have come a long way in honoring different religious ceremonies, but even talking about the power of the craft associates people with black magic, negative witchcraft.

The Broadway play "Wicked" depicts the story that the Witch from the "Wizard of Oz" was really not evil. She just had power and Glenda the Good witch really was the one that was causing harm. This theory states that Glenda was gorgeous and that she must have been good and had the most power. In today's society people still judge a woman by her beauty and she has power with this, but all women no matter what shape or size is the beholder of her broomstick that is in every kitchen. She has been taught to sweep the floor and keep the house clean, cook, and raise children. She is the master of her talents.

The Cauldron

People need to be aware of their power; the power of words and actions. How we speak creates our character. What we think, we will manifest. Thoughts carry a vibrational frequency. These thoughts travel to attain what we want.

By incorporating the four elements, earth, air, fire and water into our lives and respecting all of these nature spirits, we can begin to realize that all of life is one. The stone people or rocks have a spirit within them. They can heal.

The cauldron is an important archetype in Celtic Spirituality. It represents the womb of the Goddess and a portal to the other side. Just realizing how powerful you are helps you to believe in yourself and tap into your intuitive abilities.

I have purchased a big cauldron and keep it in my home. This makes me aware that I do have power. If you fill a cauldron with water, even a cheap plastic one that you find at Halloween and gaze into it, you may see something. This leads to an ancient art called scrying. Looking into the black hole or vortex that the water filled cauldron has created and staring at it for a long time will help you to feel powerful. If you want you can sprinkle sea salt around your home for a blessing and to keep anything negative away from you or your loved ones. This provides a feeling of safety from any so-called negative entities. But as I said earlier, the only negative energy is people.

People that are angry at you and wish harm on you can actually perform a psychic attack on you. That is why it is always good to protect yourself and imagine a pink bubble of protection around you. You can also say a prayer for the white light of the holy spirit to stay around you.

I started to work with my angels by writing letters to them asking them to help me with certain situations in my life that were bothering me. If you write a letter to your angels and believe that they will help immediately with a situation that is troubling you, they will help you right away. This can help with health conditions or just praying to the angels to appear around you so that you can see their beautiful colored lights. I continue to see my angels daily. I call on many angels to help me. There are the cherubims and seraphims, Thrones, Virtues, principalities, Dominions, Carrions or the Archangels. Michael, Uriel, Raphael and Gabriel.

Calling on Your Angels

I have called on angels to help me in many situations. I often write letters to my angels and see more proof that they are in my life to help me and to support me. Angels help people in many situations of danger. We hear stories constantly of people experiencing an angel visit in an event in their life, where they survived a near fatal car accident or some other form of danger. Some people hear a voice of warning instructing them to do something that will protect them.

When I see my angels around me, I see beautiful colored balls floating in the air. These balls of light are usually blue, pink or sometimes yellow. I feel angels come in the form of these balls of light, called Orbs. You can call on your angels anytime you need them and ask them to give you an answer to something. You may hear something on the television or a song on the radio.

Reincarnation and Past Lives

When a person dies they sometimes reincarnate into another body. This is called a walk in. A spirit on the other side decides to come back to another life and the spirit of the deceased person will enter the body of the new baby human. This can also happen with animals. If you are trying to connect with someone on the other side while doing a reading and you can't seem to get much information from this person, they may have come back into a new body.

While doing a reading for someone once, I was trying to connect with a client's mother. The only thing I kept hearing and picking up visions of was a new baby. The client told me that his sister had a new baby. I realized that the mother was not coming to me in spirit because she was already back. This does not happen often, but it does happen.

When a spirit is back in someone else's body, this is called a reincarnation. The baby will grow up and remember the past life of the mother. A memory of a spirit is called an imprint. When you try to connect with a spirit the memory of things that happened on the earth plane when they were alive registers in you senses. This is the imprint or implant that their energy has made.

Crystals

Crystals to hold for divination can be small. These will help you to tap into your intuitive and healing centers in your crown chakra. Holding a small crystal and putting it on your third eye will help to open your third eye chakra. This also makes your visions more powerful. I use crystals of all kinds and healing stones to place on different areas of my body.

Also I believe that when you are doing this kind of work, you need protection and healing. The stones are perfect for that. I have gotten a book on stones and their healing properties and when my energy is low and I need to re-charge myself I meditate and lay with crystals placed on my body. This helps to strengthen the aura also.

Protection from Electromagnetic Fields

When a person is around a lot of computers, televisions, microwaves and such, it is important to ground and protect your energy from these energy fields. A person can become irritated by all the waves of digital dharma and feel very scattered. When you walk into a room with a computer and feel it's energy currents, you will know what I mean.

Walking in nature and just slowing down from the fast paced every day life is so important to becomimg a good psychic. Meditation and prayer are the two things that I rely on the most for protection. Walking in nature and proper diet are all things that have also helped me to become a successful psychic and medium. The more you connect with the inner peace and joy and tranquility, the more you are in tune with the mystic. To mix the mundane existence with the mystical is always what I strive to do. Even walking through the grocery store can be a mystical experience if you pay attention to things, slow down and see the beauty in life. In realizing that we are one with everything and should love the whole world, even the evil people, because we are all connected.

Fear is always false evidence appearing real. When a person is paranoid of the violence in the world, what can help is to realize that they must also send love to the violent and fearful people. They are human also. The 9/11 terrorists created a lot of fear in the world, but they are also human just like you and come from a place of love and strive also to have peace and harmony in their lives. By realizing this you can let a lot of the fear go about the world.

The news on television is always about fearful things. I have just learned to shut if off and protect myself in a bubble of the white light of the holy spirit. Wrap yourself in the beauty of a small budded flower and realize that at the age of five years old everyone is in touch with spirit and knows his or her own personal truth. It is the world that tells us that we need to strive to be better. The message we hear at age five when we go to school is that we must be better than the other. In a perfect world we can act as though we are childlike before attending that school of thought; in other words coming from pure spirit, like we were before the age of five. I tell a lot of my clients to imagine themselves at age five, lonely and crying for attention. Than imagine your five year old self sitting on your lap. Tell this child that you love him or her unconditionally and that you will never let this child down.

Every day I look in the mirror and tell myself I love and approve of myself. This self help affirmation is very powerful.

Chapter Ten

Protection

In this chapter I want to talk about protecting yourself, once your intuitive abilities have come in ten-fold. You may not know how to handle the frequencies at first and they may hit you like a ton of bricks.

I started to tap into my psychic abilities when I eliminated coffee and sugar, improved my diet and exercised more. I really focused on meditating and working on the Om sound daily. I started to notice I was becoming intuitive and psychic about everything, everywhere I went. I was picking up on other peoples energies. I am an empathic person so I feel the emotions of others. At one point, I noticed that I was seeing the spirit world everywhere I went. I was having psychic dreams every night. And I guess you could say I was a little exhausted, manic and overwhelmed. I started to pay attention to the feeling of anxiety and excitement at the same time. I realized that I needed to ground myself because I was experiencing everything at once. If this happens to you I have listed some things that you can do to help ground and protect yourself, so that only when you need or want to use your abilities you can tap into it. In order to tap into your abilities before a reading I suggest meditation first. But just channeling by saying a prayer is all you really need. The prayer is as follows:

Mother, Father, God thank you for using me as a channel of your love and light. Spirit Guides, surround us now, Angels, surround us now, Thank you for giving me insight for....today.

Hold the client's hands while reciting this prayer. To protect yourself from feeling overwhelmed from the energies that you will start to experience, I suggest getting regular massages. This helps to relax you while you are transitioning into a higher level of existence. Also you need not obsess or worry about things at this critical time. Bills or mundane earthly things are not really the big picture. When you connect with spirit you start to realize that these worries are only an illusion.

While driving your car, you can ask the angels to protect your vehicle. I do this at all times, whenever I am driving. This helps so that you don't feel like the car is flying. I say that humorously, but that is what I experienced. I also had trouble going over bridges, because I did not feel grounded. To ground yourself imagine you are totally enveloped by a white light that forms a bubble around you. Imagine the bubble with little holes or tears in it, and then picture a needle and thread sewing up these rips.

The Bible

Another thing that started happening to me when I became a public psychic and medium was that people started to harass me about the sayings in the Bible and other people's religious belief systems. The Bible is a history book, written by man, inspired by God. It is one book out of many books that discusses stories that form the foundation for Christian belief systems.

I was raised Catholic so I was always afraid of the bible when I was a little girl. The nuns more or less made me feel that I should not dare pick up the bible and read it or I would surely get hit by a negative force. I don't know why I had this illusion in my mind when I was a child, but the nuns made me feel that way.

After word spread that I became a psychic reader I found myself in many situations where I had to explain myself. People were judging me from all different dimensions. I went through a long period where this happened, until I was strong enough to believe in myself. After I got strong enough, it seemed that spirit did not send those kind of people my way as much. When I went through a certain elevation period in my career, it stopped happening all the time.

In the Bible there is a chapter and verse in Peter 4:11, that talks about reading oracles. This was enough confirmation for me that everything I did was alright. Also the fact that the bible spoke of prophets quite often I knew that any distorted perception people my have read stemmed only from their own ignorance. The bible always says not to judge others, lest you be judged. I remember these words and I try never to judge anyone. Speak truth about people, but only the good is one of the Native American Ten Commandments. I firmly follow this because it makes me feel better about myself.

Patience

To be a spiritual person, you must be a patient person. Impulse thinking comes from a lower vibration. We must slow down and meditate and wait for answers to come from God. If you don't know what to do, do nothing. Let the universe give you the answer.

When my angel appeared to me she said "Patience is a Virtue." I realize that times in my life when I am not experiencing patience with myself and with situations in my life. I am not having the right spiritual feeling. We must be patient in all situations. Along with patience with other people.

Yoga

Another way to tap into your own personal truth is through yoga. When you do this regularly it helps you to connect with all the universal masters. This helped me to get in touch with visions and made me feel more at peace while I was trying to connect with the world in a different way. Yoga is so relaxing and incorporates mind, body and spirit into the workout.

I get so much out of yoga; I cannot begin to tell you how much it helps me to fulfill my life's purpose. It relaxes my body so that I am in a peaceful state so that life and its challenges are not so unbearable. I realize that life needs to slow down and be enjoyed. Yoga makes life simple and makes my thinking clear and focused.

I once had a reading from a Psychic in Lillydale. She told me that my grandfather in spirit wanted me to use self-discipline. I started to wonder if I should take Tai Kwon Do, but I decided to just do the Yoga at home with a DVD. I noticed that I did not crave caffeine as much and I did not need to eat a lot of junk. I had been an emotional eater. Yoga helped me to change my eating habits to healthier ones and to make healthier choices.

The detox yoga and the kundalini yoga are exceptionally good for me. I highly suggest detoxing with castor oil for the liver and Apple Cider Vinegar also. Drinking a lot of water and removing waste from the body is another excellent detoxing method. Eliminating meat for a while is also very helpful in getting in touch with the psychic mind and the magical self.

How to handle the energies when they come in:

When your psychic abilities increase tenfold by practicing all of the procedures in this book, more information will flow naturally on how to do it. Being able to handle the energies and go back to life as usual after you start to notice the magic and possibly tuning into your psychic abilities and seeing lights around people or entities is sometimes challenging. When you reach a higher vibration there may be challenges on the way because you are changing spiritually and growing so much that people that you used to be able to talk to, may make you angry because they are at a different level spiritually than yourself. If you are talking to a person and you realize that they are coming from a place of negative energy try not to judge them or the situation. This will start to feel good after a while knowing that the person cannot effect you or make you angry by not taking in their negative emotions.

Doing a reading invokes a very meditative, peaceful state. When I was working on myself daily as a reader I worked hard and went deeper and deeper into my psychic abilities. It is a different energy when I am just having fun being myself, cooking, cleaning and going to visit my friends. *I circulate with joy* was a good affirmation that I would say daily because I was so dedicated to the side of myself that I am a reader, that I needed to lighten up and not obsess about it. I wanted to laugh and play and still enjoy life and feel grounded. This was sometimes difficult when my mission to be nothing but the best reader possible was taking over. I would not know when to shut it down and forget my identity that way. The identity that I built around myself as a professional reader is important. Some look at me differently at times. What I have learned most is that it is not important what other people think about me, but what I think about myself is what counts.

I am very spiritual and take spirituality very seriously. You too will realize that this is a way of life. An existence that becomes your whole being. People will understand that you have changed and you will draw in more positive people when you change yourself.

Chapter Eleven

The Pet Psychic Incident

Pets are very helpful for a person to heal and to be psychic. I have a dog that was born on November 11th, a very spiritual day. She is a Yorkshire Terrier breed mixed with Poodle. She was so cute and tiny when I purchased her. Sometimes, laying in the palm of my hand, I would put my dog, Maya, on my heart or fall asleep with her on my stomach. I would feel as though she was healing me.

After a while I had developed a fear around Maya. She was taking a lot of my time and work. She kept me up at night and I was exhausted. I also developed an allergy to her fur, even though the pet store told me she was non-allergenic. I started to obsess and worry a lot about the fact that Maya was ruining my meditations as a puppy. I was very nervous that I would not do well on my readings and when people came to the door for readings, she barked and changed the energy of the calm and peaceful environment I was used to in my home.

Through many months of feeling like this and having intense fear around my animal that I loved so much, I decided to give her away because I was so stressed out. I talked to a friend of mine that loved dogs and he said he would purchase her for $300.00. I took her over to him. When I got home I cried and cried. I felt a sense of relief, but I quickly became horrified that I did the wrong thing.

I realized that night that I made the wrong choice and wanted her back desperately. I called my friend and said, sobbing, "Please Mike, can I bring Maya back?" He said of course. I felt so relieved. I went to pick my dog up and realized a big lesson: Fear blocks love. The most important thing we do on this earth is to love one another. Especially an animal. They are pure love. They bring joy and happiness to a person.

All I wanted to do was play with my dog. I realized that I did not want to work on my readings when she was small because I just wanted to frolic with her and have joy and happiness. I needed a balance. More and more I realized that the experience helped me to be more psychic. I worked through the fear and a lot of powerful things happened to me. Through the experience with my dog, I became stronger and realized what fear, obsession and worry, did to me. *I* became more empowered as a reader to help people with their problems than ever before because I had so much compassion for fear and worry. I realized that a lot of people are afraid.

Vibrations and Frequencies

Becoming more aware of vibrations and frequencies is important in helping you to manifest your psychic awareness. When you are sitting next to a person and he or she is speaking of something sad, usually you absorb some of this sadness yourself. People are naturally empathic in a way that we are aware of others people's emotions just by their body language.

When people sit down for a reading and they are looking sad and their gazes are blank and pensive, they usually look straight forward, appearing as if their houses just blew down by a wind storm and they are in shock. This look represents to me that the person is suffering from a loss of a loved one.

Body language tells the type of loss that the person is experiencing. If I feel a female energy around me and the client looks as if they have at least some closure over the death, this is usually their mother or grandmother trying to come through. When I see a ring in my third eye, this is usually a symbol for a grandmother or mother. If the ring looks like an engagement ring or a wedding ring, this could mean two different things. The ring could mean the woman is going to get married soon or is in a relationship. After a while you will be able to feel things out. You will start to rely on vibrations and frequencies around the person, to tell you if you feel they are in a relationship that is a good one or if it is experiencing some problems.

The vibrations that people put out are meters of their emotions. You can always tell when a person seems sad or depressed, happy or vibrant.

Tapping in to Psychic Abilities

Manifesting your dreams to come true as a psychic are very simple. You have to believe that you are psychic already and that you are able to connect with the spirit world. As long as you see yourself in this light, you are already manifesting it into reality.

If you doubt yourself, you will not be psychic. You have to believe that you already are, because we are all born with psychic abilities. We just need to tap into it again.

Decisions Are Never Hard to Make

You never have to worry about making a big decision. If you want to make the right one the universe gives you the knowledge of what to do. You can wait and know that you will hear the answer through other people. Or if you don't know what to do, do nothing. The answer will be very apparent at a later date.

I was deciding one day weather to go shopping or go on my daily walk. I was in a hurry and I stopped and felt that a walk would be better decision. Even though I wanted to get a lot accomplished in one day, I went out the door to go for my walk. With the thought of what I was going to buy for dinner later that day at the store, I walked outside and stood by my husband who was raking a pile of stones and gravel, by the curb. I told him, I was on my way for the walk. All of a sudden I see this little two year old boy, wheeling down the street on his big wheel. He was all by himself. He asked me if he could pet my dog. I had her with me for the walk, and I said yes. I realized that this little boy was very young to be by himself. I asked him where he lived, and he just pointed. I did not know what house he lived in, so I yelled across to my neighbor and she told me. "I think it is the house with the open garage."

The little boy had already started to wheel down the street on his fancy big wheel and he turned the main corner at the end of the street and proceeded to go left on the sidewalk. This was the main street. I was horrified to see that he was not turning back around and he was alone. I ran to the house with the open garage to tell his mom. His mom opened the door and wondered what I wanted being a complete stranger. I told her that her son turned the corner and was headed left on Electric Blvd. She had no idea that he even left the house. She ran down the street after him. My husband then realized something was not right and started to run. He found his empty big wheel in front of the school, which was two blocks away. He yelled to the mom, "I see his bike." She looked horrified and her heart sunk.

The mom by now was probably thinking someone surely abducted her son. The little boy was found in the school. He had walked into the school and someone yelled out to my husband and the mother, that he was in the building and was ok.

If it wasn't for my walk, I would have never seen the little boy. My husband would not have paid attention and kept busy doing his gravel work. I made the decision to go for my walk and it was exactly where I needed to be for the highest good, so I could help the little boy get found. As you make decisions you can pause during the day and take a brief moment to reflect on the day. This will help you in the fast paced, world we live in.

I always start my morning off with prayer or meditation. This really helps me to be able to make better decisions for myself.

Our deepest fear is not that we are inadequate; it is that we are powerful beyond measure.

It is our light, not our darkness, that most frightens us. The right hemisphere of our brain operates from pure spirit. Our left hemisphere tells us that we should buy bananas for breakfast. We are connected to everything. We are all one with the universe, the floor, and the sky; we are all one.

Never doubt yourself on your decisions, weather or not to go to the dentist for a filling or not. The universe will give you the correct answer. Just ask someone. God speaks through others. As I said, we are all one.

Chapter Twelve

Castle in Heaven Meditation

One day while looking in my crystal ball, I saw a castle and some gold glitter in the air around it. I saw a rainbow near the castle and bridges around it. I realized that I was probably seeing the other side.

I suggest doing a meditation on a castle. Your castle can look the way you would like it to. And visualize this castle in heaven, every day, for five minutes a day. I feel that by doing this, you will manifest all of your desires and create a heaven-like existence in your world. Below are instructions of how to do a guided imagery meditation using a castle as a focus:

Sit quietly in a chair with all distractions out of the room. Or you can lie down on your bed. Close your eyes and take a deep breath. Feel every area of your body relaxing and feel very safe in your little cocoon of darkness. Now picture a beautiful castle in your minds eye. As you see yourself walking toward your castle and see what your castle looks like on the outside, take note of how vast in size it is or if there is a mote or bridge around it. Start slowly walking into your castle and see all kinds of golden snow flakes falling like glitter around the outside of the castle.

Walk into this beautiful castle. This castle is your home on the other side. The castle is beautiful with a rainbow nearby. Flowers of every kind on earth are growing around your castle, and the water is the freshest spring water you can drink. You have healing herbs of lavender and sage in your healing room and all the spirit guides and angels come to visit you along with people who have already passed. You may even hear an occasional concert with Elvis or entertainers who are on the other side or receive messages from whomever you admired on the earth. The fine china and food you get imported from far away exotic places are always within your reach. Fresh coconuts and wines that are made from the finest berries are in abundance. Nothing but the finest linens are on your bed. Healing baths are in the fountain in the back yard as is your pool filled with stones of rose quarts and lapis lazuli. You never worry in your life living in your castle because all of your needs are met.

This visualization is what I think it is like on the other side. This helps you to have so much joy and peace in your life to know that life is everlasting. Carry this vibration with you at all times knowing that you are sacred and you are here for a reason: to bring others happiness.

Every situation we go through in life is good and it teaches us something. We can be grateful for every experience. Live in today's energy, getting ready for the planetary shift of awareness, by 2012, we will feel the energy pulling us to heal ourselves with touch and herbs from the earth. Caffeine and sugar and processed foods can be eliminated from the diet because they do not promote psychic ability. You will feel better and your body will remain your temple. All of the needs are here on this earth for healing, for instance, shark cartilage to heal cancer and a positive frame of mind. There are emotional reasons behind every illness and the negative belief. For instance, ear problems are caused by discontent in what you are hearing around you.

Manifest

I want to remind you in this book that every thing you want in life can be attainable. You just need to visualize it each day, and act as if it is already here. Be ecstatically happy when you feel your vibration being put out into the universe of the utmost excitement about the possibilities for your life. Anticipate that vacation to the Bahamas. See yourself getting the recording contract or a record label for songs you have written. You can manifest your dreams to come true, just like in the song. "Somewhere Over the Rainbow." Have fun, good luck and honor the magic within!

Treasure Map

To help you manifest, the instructions for making your own treasure map are listed below:

1. Purchase poster board or a frame or large piece of wood
2. Several magazines
3. Photograph of yourself appearing happy
4. Scissors
5. Glue

Cut pictures out of the magazines of things that you want to appear in your life, for instance a new car, a vacation or a new dress. Place the photo of yourself in the middle of the treasure map. Glue the magazine pictures around the photo of yourself.

You can cut out words like healed, wealthy, successful or write them in marker around your picture and the magazine cutouts. When you are done, hang your treasure map in a location where you will see it daily.

If you want an exact dollar amount of what you would like to be making per year, you can put that on your treasure map also. Be sure you believe that your map will work.

Making a Cosmic List

A cosmic list is something that you write down that you would like to show up in your life. Be specific down to every detail of what you want in your life, sort of like a New Years Eve resolution list. If you want a man to appear in your life who is a non-smoker, non-drinker and no children, that is specifically what you need to place on your list. This list can go in a special place or under your bed. This list is magical and you will notice these things showing up in your life.

Orbs

Orbs are balls of light that show up in photos. The camera flash usually catches them, due to the light. Orbs come around during parties or during travel when people are very excited about life. When you are emitting a positive frequency and vibration, the orbs usually appear. They also appear when you are in a peaceful state, after mediation or very relaxed.

You can train your eye to see orbs by noticing when one is floating in the air around you. Usually you will see it out of the corner of your eye. Some are colorful like yellow or pink and some are clear.

When I first started seeing orbs, I thought something was wrong with my eyes. They appeared as little bubbles. Like someone is blowing bubbles in front of you. They are very magical and I usually feel a very happy vibration when they appear. I am always out in nature on my walks when I see them, but I also see them in my home.

When orbs are out in nature, they are clear or white. They will show up in photograph's for instance if you are standing at the edge of the Grand Canyon. When you are very happy they will appear. You can ask orbs to surround you with their healing energy. Just emit a positive vibration of pure joy and they will come around. They are sort of like nature spirits, as we spoke about in earlier chapters.

The orb that appears in a photo on page 66, was taken in my back yard. I had built a medicine wheel and it showed up when I took the photo. This orb probably had some connection to Michael the Archangel. You can train your eye to see orbs daily, just by holding a happy vibration.

Cloud Formation

The cloud formation on page 68 was taken by a son of a woman whom I did a reading for. He sent it to her two days before he died. He was in the Navy and e-mailed it to her. The note he wrote to her was "I will always be with you in spirit." I realized after seeing this photo that we all know when we are going to pass, on a higher subconscious level, but when we get close to that point we are at peace with it. We are probably vibrating at such a fast speed before we pass that we are very intuitive even if a person is sick.

I feel that when a person goes home it is just like walking on to a new plane of existence. It is the passing transition, that is probably the hardest to get through, like the birth itself of a newborn baby. The baby goes through a similar tunnel and experiences fear and probably some pain emotionally. But the baby is protected by God so that it does not suffer too greatly.

Believe in the Magic

When I was watching a children's movie about a fairy once, I turned the television off afterwards and noticed the same fairy in my room moving around. I realized that my eyes were not playing tricks on me and that all of the children watching the same fairy film probably brought the spirit of this entity to life.

We must be childlike and feel magical about life. What do we really have to lose by this belief system? Just as Christmas time feels magical and the belief that Santa Claus really exists for children, so does it exist for adults. We have made the fantasy come alive and we feel happy when we see Santa Claus in stores and shopping malls.

The media and television can sometimes leave us feeling happy, but watching the news and negative things in the media can be quite depressing. It blocks the energy that you need to feel the life force when you watch too much garbage on the television

A friend of mine has a daughter that is thirteen. She really wanted an expensive black purse for Christmas. The purse was a designer handbag and I thought I would love to give her one, but the cost was around $300.00. As I was headed over to her home to give out Christmas presents, so I decided to make a detour to the thrift shop.

I told myself on the way there that they have to have what I was looking for. I visualized it being in the store and me purchasing the original designer handbag in the same color that she wanted, for a very inexpensive amount. When I got to the store I rumbled around many boxes of purses and found nothing. But then I went over by the cashier and there in the bottom window was the exact original designer handbag she wanted for eight dollars. I was ecstatic. I bought it for her and my friend's daughter was very happy. I was so surprised that they had the exact handbag I was looking for that it really made me feel good about the magic.

Witches, Sorcery and Wizards

Witchcraft is widely misunderstood. Witches were midwives and healers all relating to one thing; mother earth. Using the herbs and tinctures from the planet, they empowered themselves with their craft and used their thinking to get what they wanted. This philosophy goes along with the same thinking that tuning into your magical frequency can allow the power inside of you to surface, using the elements of earth, air, fire, and water and your own alchemy.

Remember, I literally turned my thoughts into gold in my story at the beginning of this book. We all are Sorcerers and Wizards, if we just believe it. We are all witches, sorcerers and wizards walking around the planet, co-creating our existence by our thoughts, words and vibrations. When people get stuck in negative ways of thinking and complaining they are literally not aware of how negatively powerful this is. If they start to pay attention to the benefits that occur when they stop complaining they will see that they are no longer creating the negative situations. It could be any situation, even if you complain that you hate watering your Mom's orchids, while she is out of town. More things will happen around the situation you complain about. You will start to notice that your mom will call you and ask you for another favor, or you get your car stuck in her driveway while she is staying in her condo in Florida.

Test your own power out and keep focusing on something. Watch that what you think of will magnify around you. Walk out of your house and pay attention to the signs and synchronicities. They are very much alive and they exist. You will see for yourself if you are aware.

That is why I say we are all little witches and wizards. We just need to realize it.

Aliens and Spacecrafts

To think there is other life out there fascinates a lot of people. There is an element of magic in this thinking that people want to believe in other sources of life, just as the belief in God exists. A lot of people want to believe that there is a force out there greater than ourselves that can come down and connect with us. This is man's way of believing in magical realms of existence. Man wants to see it for himself so he goes out and looks for it in the planets and galaxies. People are also fascinated with crop circles and the insatiable desire to find some other form of life, just as they look for the spirit of a person who has passed.

When my cousins that I spoke about in the beginning of this book, died my mom was devastated and ran all over the house crying hysterically. She did not realize that she had a spool of thread that had stuck to her and unraveled throughout the whole house. My sister and I seeing this thread started to laugh. We were young and we did not know yet what my mom was crying about. When I found out what had happened I remembered later that my cousins always laughed with me. We laughed until we were blue sometimes. I realized the thread appeared to make me laugh. To this day I still find thread appearing and it reminds me of my cousins Marcia and Mary Kay, who died when I was at such a fragile age.

Protection

A lot of religions believe in some sort of protection. This helps people to feel confident that they are safe, using forms of symbolism. The Amish people use Mendelas and the Egyptians use the Eye of Horace. This form of thinking feels comforting to the bearer of these charms.

Every religion uses some form of symbolism. The Christian religion uses the crucifix. This system dates back to the Pagan's.

It helps to believe that you have angels protecting you and watching over you in difficult situations. This method calms us and provides strength in knowing that something greater than ourselves with keep us from harm. Putting a white light around you is a great way to subconsciously protect yourself. Just imagine in your mind's eye a white light encompassing your whole body. Or you can use a cape. Pretend the cape gives you protection and visualize what color the cape is that you are wearing. The subconscious mind is very powerful when used in hypnosis. This is another powerful way to help protect you from negative thinking or addictions.

Mystical Magic and Folklore

There is something mystical about wolves running in a pack through the woods. There is a certain amount of power when we see something on television about animals and the way they live.

I saw an interview with a recent magician and he said that even though the economy was bad his show in Las Vegas was doing better than ever. Many magicians use rabbits as props which is a tradition that started many hundreds of years ago.

Movies like" Lord of the Rings" or "Tinkerbell," depict the magic that we all want to experience in life. Everyone wants to get in touch with the mystical in life even if they are afraid of it.

Children make up ghost stories when they are little and have an amazing ability to see the spirit world or earth bound spirits that have not yet crossed over. That is because they are fearless and have not experienced the fear unless they watch movies that show ghosts hurting people and throwing them down stairways or things to that extent.

When I was a child at age thirteen the movie "The Excorcist" terrified me. My Catholic school teacher told us about the movie and that it was a true story about a young girl possessed. I was afraid to go to sleep for weeks for fear the bed would shake. I had to sleep in my parents room at age thirteen, for a while. I feel that I lost a little bit of my inner magic for a while when I experienced that fear. I was young and too vulnerable to not believe that the story was true, since it was coming from an adult. But we should still honor our dark side, our shadow self and love it anyway.

Not to judge the Christian religion, but they focus a lot on the devil, saying things like "the devil will get you when you least expect it." My belief system is that the Christian people long ago made up an image called the devil or the man in the red suit, because they wanted to instill fear in people.

The Native American people were living happily on the land and did not believe in such a creature. They believed in nature spirits and the stone people and that everything had an inherent energy.

When the Christian movement came across the water to meet with the Native Americans they told them they must believe in this spirit, for it really exists. The problem is they made the devil to look like a pagan creature named Green Man who exists in the Celtic religion. He was supposed to exist in the trees and shrubs. They needed a creature that was not appealing to the eye. This is the same thing they did with witchcraft. Taking a normal person and making it look ugly or out of context, to scare people.

Again I am not condemning any religion, because people need this belief to feel loved by Jesus Christ and that he will forgive them for their sins. Studies for me date back to the lineage of Jesus Christ and the Holy Grail. The Dead Sea Scrolls say what happened to Mary Magdalene and the DaVinci Code I felt was on track with what it had said regarding all of those beliefs.

I think society is getting better and even accepting gay people. A long time ago, gay people were killed or thrown in jail. How we treated the black people in the 60's was terrible and how society treated gay people was also horrendously violent and destructive. At least today, things seem to be looking upward as far as how people treat blacks and gays. This goes back to my belief again about being non-judgmental. It does not feel comfortable inside when you judge someone. Even if someone is sick or has a handicap of some kind, it is really important to get in touch with your heart chakra to be able to identify with that person and see them as a child of God, just like yourself.

God exists in all of us, even in terrorists. Everyone on this planet feels the repercussions of treating someone badly and I feel that it effects the body and the whole well being on a subconscious level. By taking myself to a higher vibration and trying to be a good person, I feel that holding an energy of love is really the only way that we should exist.

War and greedy politicians are all making the world feel terrible, but we can change ourselves inside to a loving person and as a result, affect thousands of people in the world. Just by performing one simple act of love, we can change many lives. Doing a random act of kindness, giving a homeless person money or helping a single mom who is struggling to put food on the table all help you heal your whole chakra system and body to align with a universal plan of healing.

To connect with all of the ascended masters like Jesus Christ, we need to act like Jesus, even if it means not judging anyone for their beliefs. I tried not to judge anyone even writing this paragraph and it get's difficult when you have to respect Christians for believing in the devil, but I feel love towards them and know that they need that belief to help them.

Mugwart

When I was walking through my house one day, my spirit guides said the word "Mug wart." I know personally that mug wart is a Celtic herb that is used for divination. I was praying by my altar, as I try to do daily and I heard the word.

When I sit in front of my altar I have sacred object that make me feel my connection to the mystical and magical. I have a statue of Isis, the Goddess of magic, on my altar and I put water in front of her and put a crystal wand in the water every day and draw a circle around my third eye. This ritual makes me feel good which brings me to the subject of ritual.

When I was growing up in the Catholic church the mass was mostly repeated over and over again every Sunday and I stared blankly at the statues of Mary and Jesus waiting for something to happen. I zoned out because the mass was boring and I was waiting for something to happen. I wanted to see one of the statues start moving or crying. I needed one to come alive. My regular Sunday ritual was to me quite boring as a child, but I did have all the things I had to say memorized and remembered to kneel and when to say the right prayer or hymn. I look back on it now and I am glad I had a ritual every Sunday. I thank my parents for forcing me to go to church every Sunday and sing in the church choir. The only reason for my gratefulness is that I got familiar with ritual in my life. I honored the tabernacle that the priest stood at as sacred and remembered the smell of the Frankincense and myrrh.

Being in the Catholic religion must have affected me enough to want to embraced the rituals of the Catholic church, but I just needed to rebel, to show my creative side. This is my magic. I searched many kinds of religions before feeling comfortable and choosing the path I was on.

The vibration that musicians use in their songs and the drive to be successful is the reason for their inner magic to be lived out. The idol fantasy shows a drive to live out their musical craft and get paid all kinds of money. This is an example of, if you do what you love the money will just come. The thought process takes you to a place where you will be able to rule your world and your destiny in some sort of way.

This kind of lucky star philosophy goes into a dream that many people have when they wish upon a star for their inner desires to come true. For people like celebrities they carry out their magic and it brings them quite a bit of cash. I also respect actors and actresses who donate a lot of their money to charity, because they give a lot of themselves and their earnings to good causes. This is called tithing. When people go to church they give their money to the church and the need for this is so important. This is the same philosophy when actors and actresses tithe.

When the abundance begins to come in from your co-creation of abundance you also want to give back to the world. More comes back to you in return for doing this.

Letting in the Light

When I stare at a patch of sunlight that has come through the window and it reflects on to an object in my home and looks like a star getting bigger and bigger, this to me is beautiful.

If you train your eye to make contact with the sunlight when it comes through the window in your home and then stare at it for a long time, the light changes into green and starts to grow. Soon a growing ball of light appears and if you close your eyes and hold that vision of the green ball of light in your third eye, it will form a picture. You will see this picture in your third eye and it could change into another picture. I love doing this.

After you are finished with that, you may start to notice pink or purple colors form around you. These orbs and beams of light appear to me on a regular basis now, only because I have trained myself to see them through this ritual of staring at the sunlight prisms that come in from the window. I never stare directly at the sun, because I know it is not a safe practice. But it is safe to stare at the sun when it creates a beam of light onto an object and this is very uplifting.

One day I woke up in the morning and looked at the window. It was in January and the temperature was 10 degrees outside. But on the window there was a beautiful design left by "Jack Frost" that was so gorgeous I could not take my eyes off of it. It left little twinkling Christmas Light colors that were formed from the sunlight coming through the window. I thought to myself such beauty. Everyone else was complaining about the cold weather and how they wanted spring to come, but I had a rare day at home in my warm house just enjoying the beauty of looking at the design on the window. When you tune into that frequency of the simple things more is revealed to you. If you can be still and enjoy the beauty of the moment and stay in the power of now you will be rewarded. All we have is now. In the moment is where the true magic appears.

Cherishing People on Your Path

I always say an affirmation that I appreciate myself and others. Without other people and your magical connections with them, life would be dull. When you set up a negative vibration of anger or resentment towards a person, you must listen to your thoughts and ask yourself what you are afraid of. What emotion is hidden inside of you that you fear about that person? I noticed a pattern between me and people whom I respected; close friends. All would be well until an unexpected negative energy would arise causing me to become upset with others. Once I noticed the pattern I realized it was an issue inside myself that needed resolution. It was not caused by the other person. With this apiphone, I felt better about it.

I was having trouble with a person named Lisa and every time I would speak to her I would get angry because she had done things to hurt me. I could not even pick up the phone anymore without getting angry at her. I had been friends with her for a long time, but the relationship started to change my vibration, so it was difficult to be in her space. I found it harder and harder to be her friend.

When this happens to you after you start to change and vibrate at a higher level, you will notice that people who are coming from a negative field of energy will be difficult to be around. That is because you are getting ready to change so the old part of you is purging and you are birthing the new you. While you are in this process it is a struggle until you get to the other side of the change you are going through. When you change you will have compassion and feel for those who emit negative energy and then you may be able to speak to these people again with forgiveness. When you change your energy, you actually will see people pulling away from you to meet their vibration. They will attract like to them, because like attracts like.

Sometimes people feel their personal boundaries are being walked over and this is a difficult emotion to heal. Getting in touch with your throat chakra and imagining a blue light going to it or singing can help with any issues of communication that you may be struggling with.

One of the Native American's Ten Commandment states "speak truth about someone, but only the good." Though this belief can be difficult at times, it is quite necessary in order to elevate higher spiritually. It soon became clear to me that the more I spoke badly of someone the worse I would feel. By speaking badly of another we go back to that lower vibration and this is not good for our bodies.

Getting in Touch with Nature

Probably the best way I know to feel peace in my life is to go for a walk in nature. I am fortunate to live close to a paved trail that traverses a wooded area. I have spiritual connections with the people I see on my little trail, daily.

A celebrity and his wife live at the end of my street. The basketball player's wife and I started to notice that, synchronistically, she would always walk her dog at the same time that I walked mine. One day she opened up to me and told me that she had twin babies that died in the ninth month of pregnancy. I felt so bad for "Jenny" that I did not know what to say to her. I thought about it for a long time and I realized that she was healing something in her life and the walks with her dog made her feel good and she needed to be in touch with nature, just like me; to find healing.

This is the only way that a person can explore within and find answers. Of course there is meditation and other methods of introspection, but nature is refreshing and it is the sacred contract to the natural outdoors that I feel a person is yearning inside to connect with. People that live in the city especially need this form of connection for peace and well being. Even if a person is doing very well and living an abundant life, there are still struggles in life that are painful. But each painful quest that we experience in life brings us closer to God and we go deeper into our spiritual selves.

The Healing Energy of Water

I was walking through my house again and my spirit guides said the word "Holy Water." I had to think about what they meant when they said that and this is what came to me. When we look at water before we drink it and we tell it we love it and give thanks to the water for healing our bodies we make our own holy water. Our bodies respond positively to the good clean water that we drink to replenish our temples, our bodies. The more water I drink the more

I lose weight and feel so much better, so I continuously drink water daily; at least eight glasses a day.

You can do the same thing with food before you eat it. Say you love it and bless it. This may seem outrageous, but your body and frequency will respond better to the food.

I also keep many magical things in my kitchen like hanging fairies and little kitchen witches because these things make me feel good in my home. My home has many crystals and stones. Some are large in size, some are small. A collection of angels occupies my home and sit prettily in many corners. The reason for this is it supplies me with a feeling of inner magic. I suggest asking every day for the universe to show you the magic in today. I do this quite often and am thrilled on a regular basis as to what is shown to me.

Being where you are supposed to be, in life:

When people doubt their situations in life, they have to remember that they have created it. I spent much of my life doubting my existence, but then I remembered that I had created myself to be exactly where I was supposed to be. If I want I can also take steps to undo my creation, if I am not happy with it or it is not working in my favor. But you must be peaceful and happy in your manifestation and then let go and wait for the universe to bring it to you. Just for today may there be a peace within you, and may you trust that you are exactly where you are meant to be.

The art of letting go and trusting that you will get exactly what you want and need must be learned in order for the universe to provide what you want and need.

For a long time I was did my readings not really knowing how I was going to pay my bills from month to month. But I always knew that the universe was going to provide and that God was going to match my needs so that I could pay my bills each month. Each month it always works out my bills are paid and I have enough readings to provide the abundance that I need. I am sure that the faith of my belief does help to bring this into fruition.

Don't forget to sing, dance and bask in the sun. Be grateful for all that you have in your life for this brings in more of what you want.

Not Knowing What to Do

If you don't know what to do in a situation or it does not work out then you can do nothing until the answer is revealed. Sometimes this not knowing is a sign that you might consider the wrong thing. Everything that you do that is wrong eventually does seem right, but it is good to want to make the best decisions before going into a direction.

The universe always provides the right direction for you by giving you answers and signs if you ask for help.

If something is not working out in my favor, I ask angels to reveal the answer. Or I ask Angels to take care of it for me and it is immediately taken care of. I will start to see results immediately, as soon as I ask for help.

When a person is conflicted with a difficult decision it can create high levels of anxiety. The best thing I suggest is to lie down and meditate. Ask your guides or God to reveal the answer. You can also talk to your angels. Connect with whatever higher power you need to connect with and trust that the answer will be given.

Keeping Your Thoughts Positive

Remember to remain positive at all times. The minute you get stuck in the negative energy of thinking your whole day can spiral downhill.

I have designated crows to help me with positive thinking. Whenever I am having a bad day and really start to think badly, I will hear a crow. This is a reminder to keep my thoughts positive. I also do this with pennies. These reminders help me to stay in the power of now. When feeling anxiety about something, for instance having to give a large speech in front of people or getting ready to board a flight, it helps to say affirmations to yourself. "All is well" and "I am safe" are two of my favorites. By also staying in the power of now and not shifting your thoughts into the future of what may happen, you stay calm and can look forward to big events in your life with a quiet peace.

Reading for the Doctor

In the months I was going through a lot of turmoil trying to figure out how my abundance was going to take place and it seemed to be a slow period with readings in my home, I had an intervention with a doctor. I started reading for him on a regular basis and I realized that he was paying almost all of my bills with the work that I was doing for him. In a way I started to feel guilty that he was paying me so much money, but then I realized that God was helping him as well by giving him a wealthy client who also had more money than he had. The law of attraction takes place in business as well as in our personal lives. What we put out to people, we get back.

If you are worried that you are taking too much from people and not giving back, then the universe will make sure that you give back in some way, even if you are not clear on how you are giving back. Needing abundance from the doctor was becoming mandatory for me because I was relying on him and had spent way too much on my credit cards around the Christmas holiday. I caught someone once saying to me "all good things have to end sometime." But I was not going to buy into that belief system for myself.

The negative affirmations that we tell ourselves or tell others are very important. If you get anything out of this book, please be mindful of what you speak. What you speak, you create. This is so apparent to me from my life's situations. All we have to do is shake our little wand and say what we want and we can create it. It is that simple. We are all little magical beings living on this planet creating everything that happens to us by our thoughts. If everyone in the world was aware of this the world would be a wonderful place. You have to tell yourself, my world is wonderful, at all times.

Buying into the media and dwelling on negative things in the news is not good for us. Everyone wants to be happy and deserves happiness. It is our divine right to have peace in our lives. We have to work on finding inner peace and how we interact with others is sometimes an obstacle or a block to our inner peace. If someone does something to us that we dislike, we as humans tend to hold on to the anger and resentment for years. We would be so much happier if we just practiced compassion and forgiveness. Letting go of negative things that people have done to us in the past is the first step in the right direction to changing our lives for the better. By treating everyone with compassion and as equal, we win the game of life. If we are excited to see people and realize that we are all spiritual beings and that everyone is a part of God, we carry a much higher vibration and people can feel it and are drawn to us. We are all sentient beings and should not put anyone above us or below us.

Chapter Thirteen

A more intense method of tapping into your psychic abilities is to go out and purchase a magazine or use one that you have around the house.

I was teaching a class once and one of my students was discussing his struggles. He wanted to be intuitive but he was getting frustrated with himself, because nothing was happening. I went and got a magazine under my coffee table and closed my eyes and opened it to one of the pages while my eyes were still closed. Being that he was watching me I was feeling a little self conscious but tried not to let it bother me. I kept seeing the image of a home on the picture in the magazine and an image of a woman with my eyes still closed. I mentioned that this picture must have something to do with a house and a women. When I opened my eyes and looked the word "home" was written on the picture in the corner above a photo of a woman. I was very surprised that my guides had given me a picture in my minds eye of a home and the word written in the magazine was the word home.

I realize that my guides give me a lot of pictures that are symbolic of things and the more you get to know the symbols that your guide gives you the more you trust the information that you are receiving.

My client that I was reading for got the symbol of an hour glass with a sword penetrating through it, when I was doing his reading. He was very frustrated and was not giving himself enough time and patience to open up intuitively. At first when I saw the sword penetrating the hour glass, I did not know what it meant. After my client told me of his frustrations I realized that it was an obstruction or obstacle to his psychic abilities because he was pushing himself too much and not letting go and just allowing it to happen in his time.

Frustration and wanting things to fast are obstacles to growth and to attaining what we want. Everyone wants things to make them happy, but we always say we will be happy if we just have this new car or this new home. If we are not happy in the moment we have, then what good is the happiness we wish to receive. We must be happy in the power of now.

There Are Infinite Possibilities in Life

My Aunt once told me that every day she saw a man at work who would walk by her in the morning and not say hello back to her. But for many days and months in the morning she would continue to say hello to him, not worrying that he would not answer her back. She said he would sit in a little cubicle next to hers and always had his eyes down and would never make eye contact with people. He seemed very sad.

My Aunt always had a zest for life. She was excited about life every day and whenever I would see her she always made me smile and she loved to talk and bring things out in people. She is now seventy eight years old and still seems forever eternally youthful and has a contagious energy because of her happiness and enthusiasm. She told me that after many months, the man at her office finally said hello back to her, first with a grumble that did not sound like hello and then the next morning with a very pronounced hello. She got so happy because her efforts were noticed. She knew that someday he would break down and say hello back to her.

We as people should not give up on our conquests, even if it takes years to reach a goal. It may take twenty years to reach that goal, but with enthusiasm it can be reached in the universal plan.

Let's use the example of a poor person who is homeless. I do believe that a goal to have a home is attainable with your thoughts. A life of travel and bountiful existence can be reached. The homeless man that has enthusiasm and a goal to reach is more apt to get off the streets, than a person who has no motivation and drinks his life away.

Alcohol to me, sets up a barrier for growth. An occasional social drink is done by many, but to me it blocks you from source. Reaching your highest level or vibration to source and maximum potential is what I believe you can achieve by limiting alcohol in your life.

Sacredness and a Place as a Refuge

I suggest that everyone build a power place in their home to connect with their source. This source being like an altar makes you further develop your connection to spirit.

Materialism is so much a part of every day existence, but how beautiful would it be for a day if you lived off of the earth and just honored the land and held mother earth as sacred; to walk on her footsteps everyday as a prayer and not forget that we are gifted with the father sky and grandmother moon? These planets and dimensions around us are for more important and the stars hold clues to our existence.

Someone once asked me to explain what the star people are. The Native Americans believe that we all originate from the stars and we will go back to the stars. There is also a breed of children called the crystal children and indigo children that are very psychic and sensitive. These children are in touch with higher vibrations and can come in seeing people from another dimension or the other side. When children have imaginary friends, I believe that they are talking to their spirit guides or someone from the other side. If they are talking to an earth bound spirit or someone who has not crossed over yet, this may be frightening to them, but these type of children need to be supported and made aware of the fact that nothing will hurt them.

No entity from the other side can ever harm a person. That is my firm belief. In the movies they throw people down staircases, but in real life that just does not exist. All of the spirit form people come from a total place of love and peace. I have had enough encounters with them, that I know this to be true from my own experience.

Mercury Retrograde

The planet Mercury in retrograde does sometimes seem to affect things. When you feel you are moving in a positive direction, a retrograde can seem to set things back. My son is a musician and he started to get ready to perform out in various clubs after his album had been released. I was very proud of him working two jobs saving enough money to go to the recording studio every week and recording another song. Along with writing his own music, he writes very good melodies. His gift is his music to the world. This is his passion and he wants to live out his dream.

As he was getting ready to perform out in the clubs, he started to order things online like expensive leather gloves and he also had purchased a white hat that looked very good on him. One day while working in my kitchen I had thrown away a box that I thought was empty. What I did not realize, was that in it was his seventy five dollar leather gloves. When he realized that the box was gone, it was too late, the trash men had already picked it up.

He could not find his white hat either. It had disappeared somewhere and it seemed gone for good. I started to think about why he wanted these things so badly, but kept losing them. Just when he had gotten something he was very excited about performing in, it would get lost.

I noticed a pattern during these events, that the planet mercury was in retrograde. I started noticing other people telling me it was Mercury retrograde and that things seemed to go haywire until the retrograde was over. If you notice this happening just know that all things happen for a reason and good comes out of bad. But I also noticed the more I kept talking about my son losing things, the more it seemed to happen. The more I focused on it. The problem magnified.

He kept losing more and more things. He lost a ten dollar bill that just fell out of his pocket at work and the events seemed to snowball. He was probably so focused on the fact that he lost his gloves and could not stop thinking about it that he continued to lose more things. After this scenario he ordered a new pair of gloves and I realized that sometimes we will have struggles and setbacks. But we just have to keep on trying to think positive among life's struggles and when we turn away from them, everything will turn out alright. It is when we get stuck in the problems and unfortunate circumstances that we continue an unfortunate pattern.

Mercury retrograde is when the planet mercury is in reverse. During planetary shifts things can happen that effect purchases and large decisions we are trying to make.

If something does not work out in your favor let go of it and wait for another time. It could be that it is not the right time. Everything happens in divine order. If it is meant to be yours, it will not pass you by. The biggest thing I want you to remember in this book is what we think, we create. And by tuning into your magical frequency you can manifest your dreams and goals.

Finding Things for People

A person I was reading for once asked me where her CD was that she had lost and she wanted me to find it with my psychic abilities for her. I figured this was a challenge, but I thought I would give it a try. I closed my eyes and saw a piano and asked her if she had a piano in one of her rooms in her house. She got all excited and said yes, she did have a piano. "Do you think it is in the piano room?" I felt that because my guides showed me a picture of a piano, that yes that would be where the CD was. She told me later that week that her CD was near the piano, exactly where I had said it was. From trying so long to work on my psychic abilities, I started to see pictures in my third eye. These pictures eventually turned into visions. At first the pictures started as symbols in my third eye, but then at times they turn into full blown visions. Everyone can do this. It is just a matter of meditation and working on yourself. It may take years of meditation, but you must be patient. It will happen if you believe in it.

Tithing

Giving back helps us to create a balance in all of our chakra centers and helps to bring in even more abundance. It is so important that we give to others and not ask for anything in return. Just being there to listen or to provide a service is so important. In my business I always try to give back free readings to people who need to hear a message. In any business I believe tithing is so important, because we give back to the community.

Tithing for me even included giving my son the ten dollars that he had lost, so someone else who really needed it would find it. Purchasing something at the store can be tithing. I feel that this all if a form of giving back. When we start to bring money and abundance in, I am saying abundance because it can mean abundance in all things like a favor a friend does for you, we need to give back. All forms of giving of yourself to others is a form of tithing especially when you give your services at no cost. This comes back to you in so many ways. You do not have to analyze how it will come back. You just need to trust that it will come back to you in some form.

Stones

Stones from the earth can be very healing. The element earth is the compass point of the direction North and is very important to go along with the elements of Air, Fire and Water. When you hold a stone in your hand that is very colorful like Rose Quartz, you can immediately feel you body absorbing its energy. When you hold lapis lazuli you will feel a different energy from the cold royal blue that it radiates. This stone is helpful with communication. Placing stones all over your home is a good way to help magnify the energy in your home to feel the healing aspects of these beauties.

Below I have listed the various stones that I like to use and place on my altar to hold when I need the energy. Any issue I may be struggling with, for instance a headache, I will hold the stone for the feeling or emotion that I need to heal. If you need to bring more love into your life, carry around a Rose Quartz. This stone is a beautiful pink and just looking at it the bearer can see it's potential to heal:

Here is a list of stones and each associated issue that they can help with:

Rose Quartz	—	Love and healing heart issues
Lapis Lazuli	—	Communication and helping with the throat chakra.
Jade	—	Abundance and luck
Snowflake Obsidian	—	Fortune telling and magical rituals
Amethyst	—	Migraine headaches and improving concentration
Hematite	—	Helps with negative energy
Apatite	—	Helps with the appetite and food cravings
Moonstone	—	Helps open up the third eye and is good for divination
Tourmaline quartz	—	Detoxifies and helps the digestive tract
Pearls	—	helps with hormonal imbalances and headaches

These are the basic stones that are in a lot of metaphysical stores. There are many more stones that can be useful, but these are the ones that are basic.

Angel and Spirit Visitations

When a spirit comes to visit you, it happens when you lease expect it. It could be a deceased loved one or you may have a visit from an angel. Once while I was laying in my bed at night I got a visit from a spirit and I was not afraid of it. I think about when I anticipate a visit or am waiting for a visit it never happens. When you let go of wanting a visit from the deceased that is when it will happen. Spirits of loved ones really love when you put a candle out for them and burn it occasionally. They love when you put photos of them on the mantle or in a place in your home. A lot of spirits that come to me during readings show me a vision of something that a person has in their home like a collection that they used to have of angels or plates, or they show me a ring that was very important. These things are left behind and given to the people we love so it is important for the spirit to leave this information during a reading, like a ring or some collectible object they have passed on.

When you find a white feather in your home, this usually means that an angel has come to visit you. A white feather will just be laying there, out of the blue. I believe that the angel dropped a part of its wings, so that it can show you it has come to visit.

A lot of people remark about their angels and when I had started to see floating balls of light appear around me, such as orbs, I realized that this was also visits from angels or spirits. Usually a blue orb of light represents Michael the Archangel. Red is Gabriel and Green is Raphael. There are many angels, The list of angels that I use are Cherubims, and Seraphims, Thrones, Virtues, Principalities, Dominions and Powers. Each angel has a different function. Raphael is the angel of healing. He uses his healing wand to help you to magically help your body heal. When I call each angel around me I will see a ball of colored light coming toward me to let me know that this angel has shown up.

Writing a letter to your angels:

If you are troubled by a particular situation or worried about someone you can write a letter to your angels which will help with that situation. Just by taking a plain piece of paper and writing "Angels, please help me with _____," and specifying the person or situation, you will receive your angel's help. This is very helpful and immediately a sigh of relief will come over you.

There are many kinds of spirit visitations also. Earth bound spirits have not yet crossed over to the other side. These spirits are known to haunt homes. Spirits that have come back into another body are called walk ins.

I once knew a boy who was young and had killed himself. He was very troubled as a young adult. He had gotten his girlfriend pregnant and had killed himself after he found out about the pregnancy. When I saw a picture of his new son two years later after his passing, the boy looked just like him. I feel that he came back in another body. This can happen with pets also.

An aport is an object that a spirit has left. Also spirits who have passed and come back to visit from the other side can come in the form of their new body when they visit. They may not look the same. They will look younger and more vital. Sometimes they will come wearing an item of clothing that you will remember, like a baseball cap or something they wore a lot when they were alive.

People should feel comforted from a spirit visit. They should not be afraid. Usually I see spirits when I am in a very lucid tranquil state, I am not alarmed when I see them. If I am surprised and a little afraid by their visit, they will disappear very quickly. They do not want to startle you.

Living in the Matrix

When you transform into a spiritual being it is easier to live in the world and you will not be attracted to living in the matrix. I call the matrix the system where everyone is caught up in rushing through life, needing to have things that everyone else has. You will transcend into ways of being that will seem like loop holes to get around this feeling of existence. Things will suddenly appear easier to handle and things that used to stimulate you may not, like going to bars and listening to loud fast paced music. These are things that block out you clairaudience and hearing spirit.

Hearing your spirit guide's voice, may come suddenly when you are just waking up in the morning. You will start to notice a connection with your guide getting stronger and stronger.

Portholes and Vortexes

There are portholes that spirits travel through and they sometimes use areas of your home to make a vortex to come through. Usually I will see this vortex as the color bright teal blue. It will look like a round ball of light on the floor or ceiling area the spirit is coming through. There are many vortexes of strong energy fields all over the United States; Sedona, Arizona and Salem, Mass., to name a couple. I feel that the electromagnetic fields in these areas are strong due to things that have happened there over time in the past leaving an imprint of energy in that location. Crop circles all over the United States are talked about and a lot of people believe this is a hoax, but there may be validity to these happenings.

Living out Your Passion

If your passion is not to be intuitive or psychic you can decide what your passion is and live out that life for yourself. When you have something you are passionate about, you want to live and breathe that passion. Making a living off of your passion is a dream that many people have but they don't know how to quit their day jobs and make a living off their dream.

Putting yourself on You Tube is an excellent way of exposing your passion to the world. Everything is so internet friendly these days, it is a great way to get exposure in a large way. Simply tap into your magic first and believe that by carrying that vibration of success that you will be a hit. Your video must come from the heart and be funny or of interest to other people, even if you show your dog tricks or cooking videos. Do something that you are good at and that you get excited about. A lot of people are able to make $100,000.00 a year from You Tube, just by their little videos that they put on the internet of doing what they love. Just like celebrities, the media and exposure on television these days is where the money is. This is not for everyone, because some people like to keep a low profile and don't like public attention. But if you do like attention and being in the public eye, that is the way to go these days.

Inner peace and happiness is the greatest thing we can have. Getting excited about your life is the most important thing you can do for yourself. It will rub off on other people. Everyone is focused on making a buck these days, but just remember the secret is to be happy now, no matter how poor you are. Staying in the moment and being grateful for what you do have is the most important way to get ahead. You can vibrate your dream just by focusing on it for at least twenty minutes a day. But do not stay stuck in the future. Just come back to today and be grateful and get excited about your life.

I want to express how a happy vibration you are carrying of feeling successful is the best way to rub off on other people. By being a good listener and friend and helping others to have success is very large because it comes back to you tenfold. I know this to be true, because I have experienced it myself. The universe is a beautiful place and we need to keep telling ourselves that.

Creating Your Island of Dreams

Staying stuck in your life working and watching the television is what quite a few people complain about. You are in charge of your life. Getting out and being active and not isolating is the best way to find progress. Sitting around and claiming that your life is boring is the worst way to go unless you can draw in the people and places and events to come to you in your dwelling. All the people, places and events will come to you if you just guarantee it in your mind.

I like to pretend that I am living on an island of dreams where all my dreams can come true. This is a reality for me. There is not a single question in my mind that I cannot achieve whatever I want.

Love Is Patient, Love Is Kind

When you give to someone that you feel may be an enemy, it is an exhilarating feeling especially if you feel that the person thinks negatively about you and you don't care what he or she thinks. If people are constantly cruel to you or cruel to others, it does not mean that you have to be in their space all of the time. It just means that if you show them a side of you that is patient and kind, you are a role model for them. They may be a little stumped by your acts of kindness because they were so cruel, but it leaves a big impact in their heart, but mainly in yours.

It feels so good to be kind to everyone and non-judgmental. It is so freeing and exhilarating to give to someone who is in need of your services, but least expect it from you.

As it is said in the Bible, love endures all things, bears all thing, love is not jealous or boastful, love is not evil, love never fails.

When I think of the term love never fails. I feel that in all situations of hate, greed, and misunderstanding, apply love. Love can never go wrong. Having compassion for someone and seeing inside the reasons they may do what they do is so helpful.

I am not saying you have to be around that negative person all of the time, as mentioned earlier in this book. But forgiveness does help.

So many families do not speak to their siblings or parents because of a misunderstanding. This is the worst scenario. It is very hurtful to people when they withhold love.

Stock Market Struggles

If you are a person that invests a lot in the stock market, just remember to apply this philosophy of magic to the stock market also. So many people are worried about their stock; they panic and pull out their money when the economy is troubled. This affects the stock market by the vibration of fear that so many people were manifesting towards the stock.

We as a mass of people need to hear a message of positive thinking. When people were polled and asked if they believed in the paranormal ghosts and psychics, 48% of the population said they believed in psychics and haunting. Why not apply a little intuition toward the stock market when you get ready to invest?

Before investing, ask the universe to help you make the right decision and aim you towards the best investment for the highest good that will bring you abundance. You can do this with purchasing real estate also.

When you believe you have the magical energy that I am talking about in this book you will start to see it working in your life in all forms, even helping you to manage your money.

When we apply the elements of earth, air, fire and water in our lives and trust that the magic will take place, it is working.

The compass point for the element of Air is in the east, the compass point for the element of fire is in the south. In the north is the compass point for the element earth and the west is water. These are helpful to know when you are standing in a power place. Your kitchen envelopes these elements around you while you are doing daily tasks. I feel that this helps add to the magical thinking. It is an ancient little secret of mine that has been passed down for decades.

The great thing is in modern day times we are allowed to apply our magic. It is a free country and I am sure the new energy coming in, with the planetary shifts, will help to support people in the years to come, as far as helping small business and people being able to live out their passion.

The Large Hedron Collider

A time machine was built by scientist to use 80 million dollars worth of electricity to speed up time. If scientists can use this device to create black holes in the universe, imagine what technology can do for us. It is a prime example about how scientists have created something to happen and the money was there for them to manifest. I do believe it may have worked somehow, even though it is reported that it did not work.

What if it worked in people being able to manifest more rapidly and we just don't know?

We need to prepare for the energy changes to come around 2012. The earth is starting to show us patterns that change is imminent. Environmental changes, like eight earthquakes around Yellow Stone National Park, are the very example I am talking about even though people would argue that these things have been happening over time and that they are normal. The feeling is that there is change.

For the first time in history there is a black President of the United States of America.

If we care about the environment and make small sacrifices like not starting our cars and letting them warm up for too long in advance before we get into it and drive away, we are actually making an effort to help the environment. You will feel good about helping somehow and this catches on.

One word said to one person can travel to 4,000 people. Just imagine what one statement can say out of loving kindness to others, or one idea of something new. The inventor has one sudden idea that comes to him and he helps the lives of millions.

Self-Discipline

Everyone who wants to reach a goal in life must practice self discipline. By practicing over and over again the things listed in this book regarding meditation, psychometry, and positive thinking, you can reach your goals of manifesting and tapping into your psychic abilities and magical frequency.

When trying to reach a goal the trudge uphill can seem long, but the minute you let go, there seems to come change and a sunset waiting for you at the end of the long road of self discipline.

Having fun while you are doing the things in your life that you want to attain is the key factor. Going within and gaining inner knowledge seems to be the thing that works the best. People need time away from the loud noise and hustle and bustle of the world. Taking a day just to be with self is so important. Just by honoring yourself and needing rest and going into self care of your body and diet you will see positive improvement.

Sometimes just taking a whole day to be pensive and think of all you have achieved is good. Taking care to rest and nurture yourself in all kinds of ways, like hot baths in Epsom salts and knowing that you are working on giving back to yourself, all of the work you have accomplished will reward you tenfold.

Taking time out to get a massage or some form of healing on your body is a way to feel balanced and whole again, so more work can be done. Regular exercise or walks in the woods are great for the soul to just be idle for a while, so that you can have a state of being that is healthy and balanced.

Creating a Spiritual Relationship

A partnership between two people for a long period of time can be wonderful, but with it comes challenges. We all long for an exciting life and to have some sense of independence and freedom. But sometimes we do not co-create together lacking a spiritual harmony between two people.

Each relationship that we are in is in divine order, for we are meant to be in it. People doubt relationships and feel smothered in marriages at times, wanting to escape them to feel a sense of freedom. We must do what we need to do for our sense of freedom, but each relationship we are in is a major learning experience for both partners, sometimes triggering the deepest of all issues from past lives to present ones.

Men trigger issues for women reminding them of their childhood experiences with controlling fathers or loving ones. Women sometimes trigger issues in men as far as smothering mom memories are concerned.

Co-creating together to manifest a healthy happy relationship, and manifesting abundance takes being on the same frequency together with our thoughts of what we want to create.

Each person is born with a passion in life and relationships must not stifle the others passion. If a person feels the urge to move on from a relationship that feels stifling sometimes they will, if we have the strength to love ourselves enough.

If a person is in harmony with their partnership, this may last a lifetime together. It depends on the type of relationship people want and if they balance each other out enough to stay in the relationship. Sometimes one person is just content in a partnership supporting the others person's goals, hopes and dreams.

People who have children have a challenge because they feel the need to focus on the children's life path before their own, raising the children together and sometimes dropping their goals for their children's goals. We do not need to drop our own goals, for our children, though if we manifest it properly then everyone receives equal balance in managing goals.

People who want to have more, but feel stuck in paying bills and going to a nine-to-five job tell themselves they are stuck, but are really not. To reach a passionate goal, it can be done that we have all of it combined and pay the bills, as long as we tell the universe that is the way we need it to happen. By telling the universe I mean asking out loud and thinking it to be that way.

So many women are people-pleasers due to a learned behavior from their mothers to cook, clean and stay at home, putting their whole lives on hold. Women sometimes resort to taking prescription medication or anti-anxiety drugs because they are so unhappy. Men in these relationships seem to pontificate a father figure that was lacking in childhood for the women.

We must reach our ultimate goals of happiness and inner peace in our lives, looking forward to life eternally knowing that we owe it to ourselves to be happy and experience our utmost possible achievements. Everyone wants to achieve, even a homeless person who drinks a bottle of vodka daily needs to achieve self destruction and self pity, the bottle being his or her God.

We all have a God inside of us that needs to feel miracles. Sometimes these miracles take time, hard work and self discipline. But I guarantee that the alchemy of our thoughts is so strong that I ask you consider giving it a try to just believe in the magic that exists inside of each and everyone that reads this book.

Printed in the United States
By Bookmasters